HOMER

OTHER TITLES IN THE GREENHAVEN PRESS LITERARY COMPANION SERIES:

AMERICAN AUTHORS

Maya Angelou
Stephen Crane
Emily Dickinson
William Faulkner
F. Scott Fitzgerald
Nathaniel Hawthorne
Ernest Hemingway
Herman Melville
Arthur Miller
Eugene O'Neill
Edgar Allan Poe
John Steinbeck
Mark Twain

AMERICAN LITERATURE

The Scarlet Letter
The Great Gatsby
Of Mice and Men

BRITISH AUTHORS

Jane Austen
Joseph Conrad
Charles Dickens

BRITISH LITERATURE

Animal Farm
The Canterbury Tales
Lord of the Flies
Romeo and Juliet
Shakespeare: The Comedies
Shakespeare: The Sonnets
Shakespeare: The Tragedies
A Tale of Two Cities

WORLD AUTHORS

Fyodor Dostoyevsky
Sophocles

WORLD LITERATURE

Diary of a Young Girl

THE GREENHAVEN PRESS
Literary Companion
TO WORLD AUTHORS

READINGS ON

HOMER

David Bender, *Publisher*
Bruno Leone, *Executive Editor*
Brenda Stalcup, *Managing Editor*
Bonnie Szumski, *Series Editor*
Don Nardo, *Book Editor*

Greenhaven Press, San Diego, CA

Library of Congress Cataloging-in-Publication Data

Readings on Homer / Don Nardo, book editor.
     p.   cm. — (Greenhaven Press literary companion
to world authors)
     Includes bibliographical references and index.
     ISBN 1-56510-639-3 (lib. bdg. : alk. paper). —
ISBN 1-56510-638-5 (pbk. : alk. paper)
     1. Homer—Criticism and interpretation. 2. Epic poetry,
Greek—History and criticism. I. Nardo, Don, 1947–   .
II. Series.
PR4037.R42   1998
883'.01—dc21   97-9458
                                                        CIP

Every effort has been made to trace the owners of copyrighted material. The articles in this volume may have been edited for content, length, and/or reading level. The titles have been changed to enhance the editorial purpose of the Opposing Viewpoints® concept. Those interested in locating the original source will find the complete citation on the first page of each article.

Cover photo: Bettmann

Every effort has been made to trace the owners of copyrighted material.

Copyright ©1998 by Greenhaven Press, Inc.
PO Box 289009
San Diego, CA 92198-9009
Printed in the U.S.A.

66We men are wretched things, and the gods, who have no cares themselves, have woven sorrow into the very pattern of our lives. You know that Zeus the thunderer has two jars standing on the floor of his palace in which he keeps his gifts, the evils in one and the blessings in the other. People who receive from him a mixture of the two have varying fortunes, sometimes good and sometimes bad; though when Zeus serves a man from the jar of evil only, he makes him an outcast, who is chased by the gadfly of despair over the face of the earth and goes his way damned by gods and men alike.99

Homer, Iliad

CONTENTS

Chapter One: Homer: His Style, Language, and Outlook

Homer's special and clearly recognizable style is characterized on the one hand by his preoccupation with myths about an age of heroes who were stronger and nobler than ordinary people, and on the other by his skilled application of literary devices such as irony, simile, and direct speech.

Through the use of colorful repeated phrases, such as "the cunning Odysseus," "goddess of the greenish-blue eyes," and "his armor rattled upon him," Homer created vivid images that the hearer or reader can readily visualize in the mind's eye, making the characters and actions of the story come alive.

For Achilles, Agamemnon, Odysseus, and the other warrior chiefs of the Homeric poems, household, kinship, honor, and prestige were core social and cultural values to be defended to the death. It is difficult to appreciate Homer's epics without understanding this unique value system, in which war was seen as a necessary means of maintaining one's prestige and honor.

Although the gods play pivotal roles in Homer's epics, these works do not advocate or communicate any specific religious doctrine or agenda. Rather, they portray the gods, in a matter-of-fact manner, as superhuman entities, each with his or her own peculiarities, needs, and powers, existing as integral components of nature, along with the heavens, earth, water, air, and so forth, a view of the divine that was uniquely Greek.

Chapter Two: The *Iliad*: Its Text, Themes, and Characters

carriage, and wise and clever in thought and deed. Yet near the end of the poem she suddenly makes a decision that seems, for her, inexplicable and out of character.

   Deeply ingrained in Odysseus's character, the art of decep-tion is a gift that repeatedly enables him to overcome mis-fortune, as when, through trickery, he escapes the clutches of the Cyclops. A scholar here explains how Odysseus often uses his ability to deceive in ways that both ancient and modern readers have found amusing and pleasing.

FOREWORD

*"'Tis the good reader that
makes the good book."*

Ralph Waldo Emerson

The story's bare facts are simple: The captain, an old and scarred seafarer, walks with a peg leg made of whale ivory. He relentlessly drives his crew to hunt the world's oceans for the great white whale that crippled him. After a long search, the ship encounters the whale and a fierce battle ensues. Finally the captain drives his harpoon into the whale, but the harpoon line catches the captain about the neck and drags him to his death.

A simple story, a straightforward plot—yet, since the 1851 publication of Herman Melville's *Moby-Dick*, readers and critics have found many meanings in the struggle between Captain Ahab and the whale. To some, the novel is a cautionary tale that depicts how Ahab's obsession with revenge leads to his insanity and death. Others believe that the whale represents the unknowable secrets of the universe and that Ahab is a tragic hero who dares to challenge fate by attempting to discover this knowledge. Perhaps Melville intended Ahab as a criticism of Americans' tendency to become involved in well-intentioned but irrational causes. Or did Melville model Ahab after himself, letting his fictional character express his anger at what he perceived as a cruel and distant god?

Although literary critics disagree over the meaning of *Moby-Dick*, readers do not need to choose one particular interpretation in order to gain an understanding of Melville's novel. Instead, by examining various analyses, they can gain numerous insights into the issues that lie under the surface of the basic plot. Studying the writings of literary critics can also aid readers in making their own assessments of *Moby-Dick* and other literary works and in developing analytical thinking skills.

The Greenhaven Literary Companion Series was created with these goals in mind. Designed for young adults, this unique anthology series provides an engaging and comprehensive introduction to literary analysis and criticism. The essays included in the Literary Companion Series are chosen for their accessibility to a young adult audience and are expertly edited in consideration of both the reading and comprehension levels of this audience. In addition, each essay is introduced by a concise summation that presents the contributing writer's main themes and insights. Every anthology in the Literary Companion Series contains a varied selection of critical essays that cover a wide time span and express diverse views. Wherever possible, primary sources are represented through excerpts from authors' notebooks, letters, and journals and through contemporary criticism.

Each title in the Literary Companion Series pays careful consideration to the historical context of the particular author or literary work. In-depth biographies and detailed chronologies reveal important aspects of authors' lives and emphasize the historical events and social milieu that influenced their writings. To facilitate further research, every anthology includes primary and secondary source bibliographies of articles and/or books selected for their suitability for young adults. These engaging features make the Greenhaven Literary Companion series ideal for introducing students to literary analysis in the classroom or as a library resource for young adults researching the world's great authors and literature.

Exceptional in its focus on young adults, the Greenhaven Literary Companion Series strives to present literary criticism in a compelling and accessible format. Every title in the series is intended to spark readers' interest in leading American and world authors, to help them broaden their understanding of literature, and to encourage them to formulate their own analyses of the literary works that they read. It is the editors' hope that young adult readers will find these anthologies to be true companions in their study of literature.

INTRODUCTION

Composed eight centuries or more before the dawning of the Christian era, Homer's two great epic poems, the *Iliad* and the *Odyssey*, were the first masterpieces of world literature. And even after nearly three thousand years, their power, vibrancy, influence, and allure have not dimmed; today, they rank second only to the Bible among the most widely recognizable and most often critically studied Western literary classics. Part of the reason for their continuing appeal is that the two works encompass such a wide range of human concepts, emotions, and experiences. Indeed, the proof of their broad conceptual scope is that they have never been confined to any one literary or academic area; students and scholars examine them with equal facility in disciplines ranging from history, English, and the classics to philosophy, comparative literature, and the social sciences.

The appeal and influence of Homer's grand epics also reach beyond the limits of classrooms and academic circles. They have been translated into nearly every known language, memorized, recited, quoted, and read for both pleasure and inspiration. "Soldiers have gone into battle with lines from Homer on their lips," noted historian Ernle Bradford points out. "Statesmen have quoted [Homer] in grave debates and conferences, and poets have tried (vainly) over the centuries to rival [his] music and story-telling power." One reason that these works reach out to and connect with so many people in so many different cultures is that they capture and glorify admirable qualities many see humanity as having lost; the events of the *Iliad* and *Odyssey* take place in an age of larger-than-life heroes who lived, and often died, according to strict codes of courage, honor, and loyalty, and who interacted directly with the gods on high.

Yet though these long-dead heroes seem in some ways superior to people of later generations and cultures, they also have faults and weaknesses with which all people in all times can identify. Achilles, around whom the story of the *Iliad* revolves, is a mighty and feared warrior with unmatched courage; yet he is also vain, temperamental, and impetuous. His mix of strong and weak traits humanizes him in a way that transcends time, place, and culture. Homeric scholar Wallace McLeod puts it this way:

> In the *Iliad* the universality is that of human nature, which has not changed in three thousand years.... With Shakespeare, we are amazed that we already know so much about his characters even before they walk on the stage ... and the same effect is true of Homer. We recognize ... all ... the players in the drama and understand what makes them do the things they do. That is one reason why the poem is so moving.

The essays selected for the Greenhaven Literary Companion to Homer provide teachers and students with a wide range of information and opinion about these epics and their author's style, language, and outlook on the human condition. All of the authors of the essays are, or were until their deaths, noted historians, professors at leading colleges and universities, and/or scholars specializing in Homeric studies. Among their distinguished company: Cedric H. Whitman, called by some the dean of Homeric studies in the early to mid–twentieth century; and famed classicists Edith Hamilton and Michael Grant, whose many elegant and informative books on ancient Greek culture and mythology grace bookshelves in stores, libraries, and homes throughout the world.

This companion to Homer's works has several special features. Each of the essays explains or discusses in detail a specific, narrowly focused topic. The introduction to each essay previews the main points. And inserts interspersed within the essays exemplify ideas expressed by the authors, offer supplementary information, and/or add authenticity and color. These inserts come from Homer's epics, from critical commentary about these works, or from other scholarly sources. Above all, this companion book is designed to enhance the reader's understanding and enjoyment of two timeless tales of human heroism and adventure, works that moved English poet John Sheffield to write in 1682:

> Read *Homer* once, and you can read no more
> For all books else appear so dull and poor,
> *Verse* will seem *prose*, yet often on him look
> And you will hardly need another Book.

TALES FROM THE AGE OF HEROES: HOMER AND HIS EPIC POEMS

The first appearance of the epic poems the *Iliad* and the *Odyssey* marked the birth of European literature; and it turned out to be a singularly auspicious and momentous delivery. One might expect that works recorded just as a long dark age of illiteracy and cultural backwardness was ending in Greece would be short, crude precursors of more ambitious and developed literature to come. Yet the case is quite the opposite. The two epics are long, majestic, highly evolved literary masterpieces, critically acclaimed by the ancient and modern worlds alike as supremely brilliant in both conception and execution. To borrow an appropriate simile, at first glance it might seem as though these works emerged full-blown, in all their complexity and nobility, out of nowhere, much as Athena, goddess of wisdom and war, was said to have sprung fully grown and armored from the head of Zeus, leader of the Greek gods.

The Greeks of the classical age, the period lasting roughly from the end of the sixth century B.C. to the end of the fourth, in which Greece reached its cultural and political zenith, attributed the *Iliad* and the *Odyssey* to a blind poet named Homer, traditionally said to have hailed from the Aegean island of Chios sometime in the ninth century B.C.; but because no one could verify the particulars of his life, he remained a mysterious and mythic figure.

What *was* certain was that the classical Greeks viewed the more than fifteen-thousand-line *Iliad* and the twelve-thousand-line *Odyssey* as vital sources of literary, artistic, moral, social, educational, and political instruction, as well as practical wisdom. These works also served as a culturally unifying force. For the classical Greek city-states, which considered themselves separate nations, the epics were the common property of all Greeks, emphasizing their shared cultural identity. Homer's influence and reputation in the ancient Greek world became so great, in fact, that he overshadowed all other writers and people came to refer to him simply and reverently as "the Poet."

THE HOMERIC QUESTION

In later European societies, however, readers, translators, and scholars of Homer came to realize that the authorship of the so-called Homeric epics was not such a simple matter. In the absence of documented evidence, beginning in the Renaissance, disputes arose over exactly when Homer had lived and how he had composed these works; some scholars even suggested a historical Homer had never existed and that the *Iliad* and *Odyssey* had evolved over time with input from many unidentified poets.

Today, such disputes continue to revolve around what scholars call the "Homeric question." This term is actually a bit of a misnomer because it encompasses not one but several important questions. First, was there indeed a real, historical poet named Homer? Second, if he did exist, did he author both the *Iliad* and *Odyssey*, or was his contribution limited to one or perhaps only to parts of one of these masterpieces? Whatever portions of the epics Homer might have composed himself, are the versions we have today substantially his, or did the changes of later writers and translators significantly transform, either for better or worse, his original vision? Finally, and no less importantly, is there any credible historical basis for the events described in these poems?

As a brief overview of these events, the *Iliad* describes a dramatic episode in the tenth year of the legendary Greek siege of the powerful trading city of Troy (located in northwestern Asia Minor, what is now Turkey), an event the Greeks placed in a heroic age of their dim past. As noted scholar and translator Richmond Lattimore explains:

> It is the story of [the great warrior] Achilles; or more precisely, it is . . . the tragedy of Achilles, which develops through his quarrel with Agamemnon [commander of the united Greek forces] and withdrawal from battle, the sufferings of the Greeks in his absence, the death of [Achilles' friend] Patroclus who tried to rescue the Greeks from the plight into which Achilles had put them, and the vengeance taken by Achilles on [the Trojan prince] Hector, who killed Patroclus.

The story of the *Odyssey* begins several months after the episode described in the *Iliad.* The Greeks have sacked Troy, and Odysseus, cleverest of the Greek war chiefs, sets out for his homeland, the island kingdom of Ithaca. But when a violent tempest strikes his fleet, he is blown off course and endures ten years of wanderings during which he undertakes many exciting and fantastic adventures.

Was the Trojan War an actual event and were Achilles, Agamemnon, and Odysseus real people? Or were they merely masterful figments of a poet's imagination?

ECHOES OF REAL EVENTS

The classical Greeks certainly believed that the Trojan War and its heroes, who belonged to a race Homer called the Achaeans, were real. They accepted, classical scholar C.M. Bowra writes, "that at a period in their past . . . their ancestors had been a race of supermen, of heroes, who were endowed physically and mentally beyond the common lot and who lived for action and the glory which it brings, especially through prowess in battle." Some classical Greeks even tried to calculate the date of the Trojan War; for instance, the historian Herodotus, writing in the mid–fifth century B.C., placed the siege of Troy some eight hundred years before his own time, or about 1250 B.C.

Later European scholars were not so assured of the authenticity of the Homeric epics, however. The issue became particularly controversial in the late 1700s and early 1800s, with a majority claiming that the Trojan War and even Troy itself were mythological while a few bold souls loudly insisted that the epics were echoes of real events. The science of archaeology was still in its infancy and as late as the 1860s had not yet produced any convincing evidence that the Homeric epics had a historical basis.

This state of affairs changed dramatically beginning in the early 1870s, when a wealthy German businessman and amateur archaeologist named Heinrich Schliemann started digging into a large grass-covered mound near the coast of northwestern Turkey. Convinced that the remains of the actual city of Troy lay below, he soon uncovered a series of ancient towns built one on top of another. Schliemann believed that Troy II, the city in the second layer from the bottom, was the citadel besieged in the *Iliad.* However, later scholars showed that he was mistaken, and that the settlement in the layer designated Troy VIIa, dating from the 1200s B.C., was Homer's Troy. American archaeologist Carl Blegen, who carried out extensive excavations of the buried cities in the 1930s, wrote in 1963:

> Here then, in the extreme northwestern corner of Asia Minor—exactly where Greek tradition, folk memory and the epic poems place the site of Ilios [Troy]—we have the physical remains of a fortified stronghold. . . . As shown by persuasive archaeological evidence, it was besieged and captured by enemies and destroyed by fire, no doubt after being thoroughly pillaged. . . . It is settlement VIIa, then, that must be recognized as *the actual Troy*, the ill-fated stronghold, the siege and capture of which captured the imagination of [poets like Homer]. . . . It can no longer be doubted . . . that there really was an *actual historical Trojan War* in which a coalition of Achaeans . . . under a king whose overlordship was recognized, fought against the people of Troy and their allies.

BRONZE AGE DISCOVERIES

Proving that Troy had been a real city destroyed by fire in the period traditionally accepted for the Trojan War was only part of the picture, of course. What of the Achaeans themselves, men like Agamemnon, the commander of the siege, who the legends claimed was king of the rich fortress and kingdom of Mycenae? Did such powerful and wealthy kingdoms as those Homer described in his epics actually exist in Greece in this early era? Here, Schliemann again led the way. In the mid-1870s he switched his attentions from Troy to the site of Mycenae, in southeastern Greece, where he created a sensation by unearthing royal graves loaded with jewels and golden artifacts in the ruins of a huge fortified palace.

An intriguing new picture of Greece in the Bronze Age emerged from the discoveries made by subsequent expeditions led by Schliemann and later scholars. This period, in which people used tools and weapons made of bronze, an alloy of copper and tin, lasted from about 3000 to 1100 B.C. Archaeologists revealed that Mycenae and other similar towns ruled by kings living in imposing fortress-palaces dominated mainland Greece and the Aegean sphere during the last four hundred years or so of the Bronze Age. Because Mycenae was both the most important of these kingdoms and the first to be thoroughly excavated, scholars dubbed this early Greek culture Mycenaean; and the period of the late Bronze Age in which it flourished, corresponding to what the classical Greeks called the Age of Heroes, became known as the Mycenaean age.

That these Mycenaeans, Homer's Achaeans, were organized, sophisticated, and powerful enough to have crossed the Aegean Sea in force and mounted a large-scale siege operation on a foreign shore is attested to by the size and splendor of their fortress-palaces. The citadel at Tiryns, a few miles south of Mycenae, is a typical example. The palace was protected by an outer wall constructed of gigantic blocks of stone; these blocks were so huge that when the classical Greeks saw some of them protruding from the ground they thought they could only have been built by the Cyclopes, mythical giants with enormous strength. Historian Michael Wood offers this description:

> Tiryns gives a particularly vivid impression of the world of the Bronze Age warlords: the ascent up the ramp to the main entrance, flanked on the right by an immense tower of Cyclopean stones, and on the left by corbelled [bracket-supported] galleries to give covering fire; the massive entrance passage leading to a main gate which must have looked much as the Lion Gate at Mycenae; then the colonnaded outer hall and courtyard which led into a magnificent columned inner court facing the royal hall, the megaron (royal hall) with its porch, anteroom and throne-room; the throne-room itself with a large circular hearth in the center, its walls decorated with alabaster [a fine-grained, white, slightly translucent mineral] and inlaid with a bordering of blue glass paste.

A comparison of this palace in its original glory with Homer's descriptions of palaces from the Age of Heroes is striking. In the *Odyssey*, he paints the following word picture of the lost Odysseus entering the "great mansion" of King Alcinous:

> Again and again he stood still in wonder, before he set foot on the brazen threshold. For a brightness as of sun or moon filled the whole place. Round the courtyard, walls of bronze ran this way and that way, from the threshold to the inner end, and upon them was coping [layer or border] of blue enamel.

SCHOLARSHIP REVEALS THE WORLD OF ACHILLES AND ODYSSEUS

Another impressive piece of evidence for the Mycenaeans' highly civilized lifestyle was their literacy. Archaeologists have found in the ruins of their palaces many stone tablets bearing an archaic script known today as Linear B. Its eighty-seven signs form a syllabary, or group of characters each of which stands for a syllable, as opposed to an alphabet, in which each character stands for a specific sound. No Mycenaean literature has yet been found. For the most part, the Linear B tablets contain long inventories of possessions, documents about land ownership, military orders, lists of local residents and their allotted tasks, and the like. We learn, for instance, the size of an estate owned by a man name Alektruon, how much he paid in taxes, and the worth of his offerings to the gods; how many slaves Korudallos owned and the tasks he assigned them; the number of sons the weaving women of Tinwato bore to the rowing men of Apunewe; that the palace's share of Dunios's harvest was 2,220 liters of barley, 526 of olives, 468 of wine, 15 rams, 12 pigs, and other assorted livestock; and that the names of Tazaro's oxen were Glossy and Blackie. Though rather dry and monotonous, these bureaucratic documents are valuable for what they reveal about Mycenaean social structure, farms, crops and livestock, tools and utensils, weapons, ships, and other aspects of daily life.

The Linear B tablets have also revealed the Mycenaeans' true ethnicity and relationship to later Greeks, which has had a dramatic impact on modern studies of Homer. For decades, a majority of scholars believed that the Mycenaeans were non-Greeks and that Greek-speaking peoples did not gain ascendancy in the Aegean sphere until the collapse of Mycenaean civilization in the twelfth century B.C. According to this scenario, Homer had taken an old surviving non-Greek myth about a war, assumed that its heroes were Greeks, and accordingly dressed it up with the names of Greek people and gods.

But in 1952 a brilliant young English architect and amateur linguist named Michael Ventris overturned this view by proving conclusively that the Mycenaean script was a very old form of Greek. His discovery showed that the Mycenaeans were in fact early Greeks, which meant that Homer had inherited, rather than invented, many of the names and words in his poems and that the world he depicted—one of kingdoms and fortresses ruled by powerful warlords—was indeed a Greek one. "The world of Agamemnon and Achilles and Odysseus," writes noted scholar M.I. Finley, summing up what historians have learned since Schliemann's time,

> was one of petty kings and nobles, who possessed the best land and considerable flocks, and lived a seigniorial [feudal]

existence, in which raids and local wars were frequent. The noble household [not unlike a medieval lord's manor] was the center of activity and power. How much power depended on wealth, personal prowess, connections by marriage and alliance, and retainers [servants and followers]. . . . The king . . . was judge, lawgiver and commander, and there were accepted ceremonies, rituals, conventions and a code of honor by which nobles lived, including table fellowship, gift-exchange, sacrifice to gods and appropriate burial sites.

SURVIVING THE GREEK DARK AGE

Having established that there was a historical basis for the Trojan War and the Greek rulers who fought it, logically the next part of the Homeric question to examine is Homer himself. Specifically, what was his and his society's relationship, if any, to the Mycenaeans; when did he live; what knowledge of prior ages did his own age inherit; and by what process did he compose the *Iliad* and the *Odyssey*?

Historians are fairly confident that the Trojan War took place in the mid-to-late thirteenth century B.C., a dating that stunningly confirms Herodotus's reckoning of 1250 B.C. for the event. Modern research also suggests that the war was one of the last, if not *the* last, of the major military expeditions launched by the Mycenaean warlords. Recent evidence suggests that they began to fight among themselves, burning one another's palaces; then, sometime in the twelfth century B.C., suffered further destruction as a less culturally advanced and very warlike Greek-speaking people known as the Dorians swept down from what is now extreme northern Greece. The key to the Dorians' success was their use of iron weapons, which were much stronger and more effective than the Mycenaeans' bronze spears and swords.

Most of the Mycenaeans who survived the Dorian onslaught fled eastward across the Aegean and settled along the coasts of Asia Minor, a region the Greeks later came to call Ionia. There, they attempted to carry on their old ways. But this effort was in vain. Their writing, government organization, highly developed recordkeeping, arts, handicrafts, and even their cultural identity rapidly faded and vanished; and by 1100 B.C. the Greek world had slipped into a dark age of illiteracy and poverty in which isolated communities of farmers, fishermen, and shepherds struggled to maintain a meager existence.

During this dark age, which lasted for some three hundred years (and about which scholars still know very little), the Greeks, former Mycenaeans and Dorians alike, more or less forgot their heritage and began to identify only with the particular valley or island where they lived. This marked the birth of the highly individualistic city-states that would later dominate classical Greece. Yet though Greece's past history had been lost, memories of some its great figures and their deeds survived as oral narratives passed from one generation to the next. As time went on, the tales of the long-past golden age, the Age of Heroes, were embellished; and roving minstrels, bards known as *aoidoi*, began memorizing them and reciting them on special occasions, all the while embellishing them further.

At first, the minstrels probably retold dozens or even hundreds of these small epics, tales not only about the heroes of the Trojan War, but also about other prominent Achaeans now forgotten. Eventually, however, a handful of stories emerged as the most important and well known throughout the Greek world. Classical scholar and archaeologist Robert Flacelière writes:

> One of these minstrels who may have been born at Smyrna [on the coast of Ionia] and lived at Chios ... [perhaps] between 850 and 750 [B.C.], more than three centuries after the fall of Troy, was a poet of genius. It was he who had the idea of isolating from the huge cycle of epics relating to Troy and treating separately two episodes that seemed to offer subjects of outstanding significance, the wrath of Achilles and the return of Odysseus. According to ancient tradition, this poet was Homer.

TRANSMITTED BY MEMORY

Thus, Homer appears to have been part of an ongoing oral tradition that both preserved and built upon tales of the Age of Heroes. Later ancient scholars were well aware of this oral mode of transmission for the great epics, as evidenced by these comments by the first-century A.D. Jewish historian Josephus:

> Throughout the whole range of Greek literature no disputed work is found more ancient than the poetry of Homer. His date, however, is clearly later than the Trojan War; and even he, they say, did not leave his poems in writing. At first transmitted by memory the scattered songs were not united until later; to which circumstance the numerous inconsistencies of the work are attributable.

By inconsistencies, Josephus meant slight variations from one telling or version to another. In the following account of how oral poets work, C.M. Bowra explains how such variations are a natural and inevitable part of the process:

> The oral poet works quite differently from the poet who writes. Recitation is his only means of making his work known, and his first duty is to keep his audience's attention at all costs. If he bores or confuses them, he loses their interest and, with it, his source of livelihood. His technique, which comes from generations of practiced bards, tells him what to do. Above all, he must not allow his story to become too complicated; he must deal with one and only one thing at a time, with all the clarity and firmness of outline of which he is capable. This means that he sacrifices much that the writer of books thinks indispensable. In oral art the moment a theme has done its task it is dismissed without ado, and no attempt is made to tidy the loose threads. The need to stress the special character of each dramatic occasion may lead to inconsistencies with what is said elsewhere. . . . Oral poetry has its own rules, which are well known to us from a large mass of poems collected from many parts of the world where the art is still vigorous and popular. It is by the standards of this art that Homer must be interpreted and judged.

Because this oral tradition encompassed many other epics and shorter poems about the Age of Heroes besides the *Iliad* and the *Odyssey*, a number of later, but still ancient, scholars expressed confusion over their authorship. Several were attributed to Homer himself, but trying to sort out which were his and which were not constituted the ancient version of today's Homeric question. In time, ancient scholars grouped these various works by subject into "cycles"; for example, there was a so-called Theban cycle that dealt with legends about the city of Thebes and its first rulers and a Trojan cycle that included various stories about the Trojan War.

THE TROJAN EPICS

The *Iliad* and the *Odyssey* were the most famous parts of the Trojan cycle, of course, and also the only ones that have survived intact. We know a little about the others from brief surviving fragments or from quotes and summaries in the works of various ancient writers who had read them or heard them recited. The *Cypria*, for example, covered the events leading up to the war, as well as some of its early stages, including how the Trojan prince Paris ran off with Helen, wife of the Greek king Menelaus, and how Menelaus asked his brother Agamemnon and other Greek rulers to form a coalition against Troy to get Helen back.

The *Iliad*, dealing with episodes in the tenth year of the siege, sequentially followed the *Cypria*, and other epics in the Trojan cycle then followed the *Iliad*. Among these were the *Aethiopis*, in which, following the funerals of Hector and Patroclus, Paris kills Achilles and the Greek leaders Odysseus and Ajax contend for possession of Achilles' armor; the *Little Iliad*, in which Ajax commits suicide after failing to win the armor, the Greek hero Philoctetes kills Paris, and Odysseus devises the idea of the Trojan horse; the *Sack of Troy*, in which the Trojans drag the huge wooden horse into their city, and Greek warriors hiding inside the horse climb out and open the gates to their army, sealing Troy's fate; the *Homecomings*, various accounts of the returns of the Greek leaders (except for Odysseus), including that of Agamemnon to Mycenae, where he is murdered by his wife; the *Odyssey*, the saga of Odysseus's wanderings; and the *Telogony*, which relates the adventures of Telogonus, Odysseus's son by the sorceress Circe, in the years after Odysseus made it home to Ithaca.

Most ancient scholars eventually decided that of all these epics only the *Iliad* and *Odyssey* belonged to Homer; and modern scholars not only agree with this conclusion, but also believe that all of the others were composed after Homer's time, probably having been inspired by his works. According to Richmond Lattimore:

> The Cycle is post-Homeric, and this can be said positively. In the first place, ancient tradition on this point is firm and unanimous. But the conclusion can be defended from analysis. If there is any character of the cycle as a whole which is indisputable, it is the businesslike manner in which the story is told from beginning to end, without gaps. But if Homer had come later than the Cycle, there would have been such a gap, for there would have been no account either of the anger of Achilles or the death of Hector, nor of the homecoming of Odysseus, since this was apparently not part of the *Homecomings*. But if the *Iliad* was already there before the Cycle began, all is clear. The author of the *Cypria* took the story up to the beginning of the *Iliad*, then stopped short; and the *Aethiopis* obediently picks the story up again immediately after the point where the *Iliad* closes.

The exact dates of most of the non-Homeric epics in the Trojan cycle remain uncertain; but it is safe to assume that at least some of them were composed before writing had become widespread once again in Greece, and therefore that they were initially passed along orally by wandering bards.

COMMITTING HOMER TO WRITING

Eventually, of course, someone committed the epics, including the *Iliad* and the *Odyssey*, to writing. When, exactly, this occurred is unknown and constitutes one of the central problems of the Homeric question. Sometime in the late eighth century B.C., with the dark age over and prosperity returning to the Aegean sphere, the Greeks became literate again. This time they adopted a set of letters used by the Phoenicians, a highly civilized and successful Middle Eastern trading people. This alphabet had twenty letters, all consonants, to which the Greeks added vowels, producing a simple yet highly flexible and useful means of recording their elegant and expressive language.

A number of scenarios for how the Homeric epics were written down are feasible. Homer might have done so himself, since it is possible that he was still living when writing was coming back into fashion; or, if he was illiterate, he might have dictated them to a scribe. However, no evidence presently exists to support either case. It is also possible that other *aoidoi* like himself, carrying on the age-old tradition, memorized the poems and then wrote them down after his death. In fact, a society or fraternity of these bards, who called themselves the Homeridae, or "sons of Homer," flourished on Chios, his home island, beginning in the late eighth century, probably not long after he died. Although these men claimed actual descent from Homer, it is far more likely that they were fervent devotees who looked upon him as their great father figure and artistic patron. Unfortunately, there is no way to know if any of them committed the *Iliad* and *Odyssey* to parchment, for if they did so the documents have long since been lost.

THE HOMERIC EPICS IN ATHENS

The most popular tradition, one at least partially documented, is that the first written versions of the Homeric epics appeared in the sixth century B.C. in Athens, which had become the largest, wealthiest, and most culturally advanced of the Greek city-states. By this time writing was widespread in Greece. Because literature could be easily and routinely recorded on papyrus and in this form used and dispersed as desired, the need for and interest in oral poetry began to wane. And as the volume of oral poetry declined, skilled bards became increasingly scarce, with the inevitable result that the art form's level of creativity also declined. Undergoing fewer and fewer substantial revisions, by the early sixth century B.C. the oral texts of the *Iliad* and *Odyssey* had taken on more or less fixed forms.

The tellers themselves were now known as rhapsodes (*rhapsodoi*), professional reciters who often competed with one another and made at least a modest living from their oral performances. Plato's dialogue *Ion*, in which the philosopher Socrates converses with his friend, the rhapsode Ion, reveals valuable insights about these men and their art, as well as the names of some of the best known of their number.

> SOCRATES: I have often envied you reciters that art of yours, Ion. You have to dress in all sorts of finery, and make yourselves as grand as you can, to live up to your art! And you are, at the same time, bound to spend your time on no end of good poets, especially Homer, the best and most divine of all poets. ... The reciter must be the interpreter of the poet's mind to the audience; and to do this, if he does not understand what the poet says, is impossible. So all that very properly makes one envy.
>
> ION: Very true, Socrates. At least I found this myself the most troublesome part of the art; and I believe I can speak on Homer better than any other man alive. Not Metrodoros of Lampsacos, not Stesimbrotos the Thasian, not Glaucon, nor anyone else who ever was born could utter so many fine thoughts on Homer as I can.
>
> SOCRATES: I'm glad to hear it, Ion, for it is clear you won't mind giving me a show.
>
> ION: I will most certainly. You'll find it a treat to hear, Socrates, how finely I have decked out Homer! I believe I've earned a golden crown from the Homer Association [the Homeridae on Chios].

Men like Ion gained widespread popularity reciting the Homeric epics and other works at religious festivals and other important gatherings in Athens and surrounding communities. In 566 B.C., the famous Athenian administrator and lawgiver Solon (or perhaps another leader named Pisistratus) brought the *rhapsodia*, the contests among rhapsodes, to the greatest of all Athenian festivals, the Panathenaea, honoring the city's patron goddess Athena. The high level of respect Homer had by then attained is shown by the fact that only his works were allowed at the Panathenaea. In 534, the *rhapsodia* also became a regular feature of the City Dionysia, a lavish drama festival honoring the fertility god Dionysus. In this setting, which eventually became the showcase for great playwrights such as Aeschylus and Sophocles as well as for Homer, the Homeric recitations became more spectacular, with full choruses backing up the rhapsodes.

Sometime during this period (the exact date is unknown), the tyrant Pisistratus evidently went a step further and ordered that the *Iliad* and *Odyssey* be written down. His motivation is not hard to fathom: to secure for Athens the prestige of having produced the first and definitive written versions of the Greek world's greatest literary works. Supposedly, he commissioned a group of scholars and scribes to complete the task. They no doubt called upon leading rhapsodes to recite for them and, for the last word in authenticity, may also have invited some of the highly respected Homeridae to make the journey from Chios to Athens.

DIFFERING EDITIONS AND TRANSLATIONS

It must be emphasized that this Athenian version of how the epics were written down may be partially or even totally inaccurate and that scholars continue to debate this aspect of the Homeric question. Yet whatever Pisistratus's actual role might have been, there seems little doubt that written versions of Homer's poems did exist in his time; therefore, the mid-to-late sixth century B.C. is the latest acceptable period for their first written forms.

Writing the epics down standardized them to a large degree, although some copies undoubtedly continued to be embellished and otherwise edited by enterprising scholars who thought themselves capable of improving on Homer. One often-cited piece of evidence for this is the following excerpt from the first-century A.D. Greek writer Plutarch's biography of the fifth-century B.C. Athenian leader Alcibiades:

> Once, when he was past his boyhood, he went to a schoolmaster and asked him for a volume of Homer. When the teacher said that he had none of Homer's works, Alcibiades struck him with his fist and went off. Another teacher said that he had a copy of Homer which he had corrected himself. "What," Alcibiades exclaimed, "are you teaching boys to read when you know how to edit Homer? Why aren't you teaching young men?"

As time went on, many ancient scholars worried that such arbitrary and often unskilled tinkering with the Homeric texts might eventually dilute and destroy them. This concern led a group of Greek scholars working in Alexandria, Egypt, in the third and second centuries B.C. to mount a massive effort to produce a definitive version that captured the originals as closely as possible. They compared, collated, and edited the many renditions of the texts then in circulation; and the result of their work is substantially the version that survived into medieval and modern times.

It is important to realize, however, that the Alexandrian scholars created the definitive *Greek language version* of Homer's works, and that the epics continued to undergo minor alterations over the centuries as they were translated into other languages. Even different translations in a single language can feature substantial variations in clarity, color, and overall effect. Take, for instance, the dramatic moment in which Achilles, having sparred with Hector, deals him the final deathblow. Richmond Lattimore's renowned translation reads:

> He was eyeing Hector's splendid body, to see where it might best give way, but all the rest of the skin was held in the armor, brazen and splendid, he stripped when he cut down the strength of Patroclus; yet showed where the collar-bones hold the neck from the shoulders, the throat, where death of the soul comes most swiftly; in this place brilliant Achilles drove the spear as he came on in fury, and clean through the soft part of the neck the spearpoint was driven.

Classical scholar W.H.D. Rouse translates the same passage this way:

> He scanned Hector with ruthless heart, to see where the white flesh gave the best opening for a blow. Hector was well-covered with that splendid armor which he had stripped from Patroclus, but an opening showed where the collar-bones join the neck to the shoulder, the gullet, where a blow brings quickest death. There Achilles aimed, and the point went through the soft neck.

It is clear that both versions cover the same basic points; however, the word usage and tone differ considerably and the reader must judge for him- or herself which is more moving and effective. Reading the passage in the original Greek renders color and tone appreciably different from (and arguably more effective than) either of these English versions; and it is tantalizing to wonder how different the same excerpt might seem in a translation made two thousand years from now in a language that has yet to evolve.

LIKE THE LEAVES OF THE TREES

It is not inconceivable that Homer's works will indeed still be read and studied two thousand years hence. After all, close to three thousand years have elapsed since they first appeared and the rigors of time, editing, translation, and seemingly endless reinterpretation have not in the least dulled their luster. The stories and characters of the *Iliad* and the *Odyssey* continue to reach out to all those who marvel at legendary golden ages long past, when mighty gods walked the earth and larger-than-life human beings lived and died for honor. Nostalgia for the faded glories Homer described and a burning fascination for the mysteries surrounding his own life and genius will likely pass from one generation to another as long as his epics survive, whether in written or oral form. "That is why the Homeric question still stands, with the other great questions of literature and history," comments Homeric scholar Sir John Myres,

> and with the greater questions of the other sciences, outside the limit of finality. There is always something new to be learned about Homer; like the leaves of the trees, critic falls after critic, theory after theory, and school after school. . . . It is we, and our tools and methods, that change, not the genius of Homer nor the perennial humanity of [his] poems.

CHAPTER 1

Homer: His Style, Language, and Outlook

READINGS ON
HOMER

Homer's Epic Style

Jasper Griffin

As a literary form, epic poetry has a style all its own.
Epic poems are usually long, grand in thematic
scope, and constructed using a wide variety of
literary devices; in these respects Homer's works are
no exception. What sets Homer apart from all other
epic poets and determines his unique style are his
choice and mix of particular devices and the special,
characteristic ways he employs them. In this essay,
Jasper Griffin, Fellow of Balliol College at Oxford
University and respected authority on Homer,
discusses some of the hallmarks of Homer's style,
including the grandeur and realism of his poems
and devices such as simile, irony, direct speech, and
parataxis, the mixing together of clauses and phrases
without the use of coordinating conjunctions.

The most frequently mentioned feature of Homeric style in
antiquity is its elevation. Epic and tragedy were regarded as
the highest forms of poetry, which presented suffering and
death in noble language and illuminated in a worthy manner
the nature of the world and the dealings of the gods with
mankind. The stories are set in a past which is felt to be both
different and special. Heroes then were greater and stronger;
heroines were beloved by gods and bore them god-like children; above all, the gods intervened visibly in events, mixing
with men and speaking to them. Heroic myth in high poetry
makes the world transparent, allowing us to see the divine
workings which in ordinary events are concealed. That is
why not only epic but also tragedy is concerned with those
myths: they allow a privileged insight into the hidden patterns of life.

Such actors and such events needed a style and diction to
match. The style of Homer is not pompous or slow-moving;
its oral and formulaic origin tends to make each line a unit

in itself, often extended by run-on (enjambement), but radically different in movement from, say, the opening lines of *Paradise Lost*, although [its author, seventeenth-century English poet John] Milton of course has the Homeric openings in mind:

> Of Man's First Disobedience, and the Fruit
> Of that forbidden Tree, whose mortal taste
> Brought Death into the World, and all our woe,
> With loss of Eden, till one greater Man
> Restore us, and regain the blissful Seat,
> Sing Heav'nly Muse . . .

No verb until line six, and no full stop until line sixteen. Such solemn density is not Homeric. The elevation of Homer is achieved by a number of devices: the recurrent and dignified epithets, the general avoidance of vagueness in expression, the firm control of varying pace and movement, the objective tone in which events are narrated, the exclusion of 'low' words and motives. This last must however immediately be qualified. Homer describes a dog dying on a dunghill, full of fleas; he tells us about a punch-up between two beggars with a couple of blood-puddings as a prize; he retails the insults of an offensive servant—'Here's one bit of bad news bringing another! True enough, God makes birds of a feather flock together. Where are you taking this man, you miserable swineherd?—This pest of a beggar, who will stand and rub his back on the doorposts—'. Napoleon, always on his dignity, was shocked by the punch-up with the beggar Irus, and none of those passages, which could easily be multiplied, can be imagined in the *Aeneid* [by the Roman epic poet Virgil] or in Milton. . . . Homer is not afraid of the natural, and he is confident that his style will raise the humble rather than being dragged down by it.

THE UNCHANGING WORLD OF NATURE

Here is an unstressed passage of the *Odyssey*, to show how routine events are handled in a style which is essentially simple. It describes the embarkation of Telemachus for his journey:

> They brought all the gear on the well-benched ship and set it down, as the dear son of Odysseus had told them. Then Telemachus went on board the ship; Athena went first and sat down in the stern. Beside her Telemachus took his seat. The men untied the stern-ropes, went aboard, and sat at their benches. Grey-eyed Athena sent them a following breeze, a

fresh west wind, sounding over the wine-dark sea. Telemachus
urged on his men, ordering them to handle the tackling, and
they obeyed the order. They stepped the mast of pine in the hollow mast-box and set it up, and fastened it to the forestays, and
lowered the white sails with plaited leather ropes. The wind
bellied out the middle of the sail, and the water resounded
loudly, foaming round the keel as the ship went on. They fastened the tackle, and in the swift black ship they set up bowls
brimming with wine, and poured libations to the immortal
gods who live forever, but most of all to the grey-eyed daughter of Zeus. All through the night and the dawn the ship went
cleaving her way.   (2.414–34)

Such a passage is not meant to surprise, except in as far as a
midnight launch was unusual (ancient sailors in those narrow and dangerous seas generally preferred to beach their
ships at night). The 'wine-dark sea' is a traditional English
rendering of the Greek phrase *oinopa ponton*, literally 'the
wine-faced sea', which probably refers to the sparkling bub-
bles on the surface, resembling those seen as one raises a
beaker of newly poured wine: the ancients did not drink out
of glass. In any case it is a regular Homeric phrase, and the
fact that this time it is dark and the sea visible in an unusual
way makes no difference. The two lines describing the sail
bellying and the water resounding round the keel recur
identically at *Iliad* 1.481–82, yet here they are beautifully appropriate, and the poet was content without trying to outdo
them. The point of the passage as a whole is its peace and
order, a welcome relief after the disorder and conflict on
Ithaca. Outside the claustrophobic setting of Odysseus'
house there is the unchanging world of nature: the anarchy
of the Suitors is contrasted with the unchanging discipline of
sailors. And we contemplate the ship, manned by its obedi-
ent crew, moving on through the darkness, amid the sounds
of wind and water, natural yet (in this heroic world) god-
given. The objective manner and the recurrent phrases,
which suggest the regularity of it all, fit effortlessly with
such effects.

A NEW START FOR THE HERO

That passage can be compared with another, more intense,
also describing the launching of a ship by night. Odysseus,
after all the perils he described in Books Nine to Twelve, has
finally reached the point where the Phaeacians will take
him home. We have just heard how he 'kept turning his head

to the blazing sun, yearning for it to set', as he waited for the evening, when they are to sail; he was as glad to see the sun go down as a man who has all day been ploughing and who now heads for his supper, 'and his knees tremble as he goes'. A bed is laid out for the hero in the stern:

> He came on board and lay down in silence, and the crew sat each at his bench in order, and they untied the hawser from the stone capstan. Then swinging back they began to fling up the salt water with the oar; and on his eyelids there fell sweet sleep, unbroken and delightful, most like to death. As for the ship: as when four stallions draw a chariot on flat ground, all lunging together beneath the blow of the lash, and rising high they speedily make their journey—even so would her stern rise, and behind her seethed the heaving wave of the ever roaring sea. The ship ran steadily on; not even a hawk could keep pace, the swiftest of flying things, so fast was her run as she cleft the waves of the sea, bearing a man like to the gods in planning, whose heart had endured much suffering in time past, threading his way through warring men and cruel sea; now he slept deeply, forgetting all he had suffered. When the star rose that is brightest, which especially comes to announce the light of early-rising Dawn, at that time the sea-going ship touched at the island.   (13.75–95)

At once we observe that the purely standard features of launching and sailing have been much compressed. The elements of normality are still there—the ropes which must be untied before the ship can leave, the oarsmen flinging up the salt water—but the focus is on Odysseus and his sleep. As so often in the Homeric poems, at a high point in the narrative the words and phrases used for the action do not change, but special novelty and emphasis are introduced by a striking comparison (the chariot bouncing over the plain) and by an unusual point of reference (the hawk in flight). The poet pauses in his narration to linger in pity and sympathy on the sleeping figure of his hero, released for a short time from tribulations past and future. In so deep a sleep he can cross from the non-human world of the Phaeacians and the Wanderings and return to real life and a fresh set of problems. 'A man whose heart had endured much suffering' in war and on the sea strongly recalls the opening words of the poem—a man of many wanderings and much suffering. It is hard not to see a conscious echo here, and a hint that this is a new start for the hero: so striking a passage, at such a point in the poem, makes it plausible that an oral audience would have been expected to catch that echo.

THE PACE OF THE ACTION QUICKENS

Another high point in the poem, this time in an active rather than a passive mood, is the moment when Odysseus finally gets the great bow into his hands. Unhurried, he turns it and inspects it, in case it has been gnawed by worms: the Suitors jeer—'I suppose he's got bows like that at home—perhaps he's planning to make one—'

> So spoke the Suitors: but Odysseus of many plans, as soon as he had handled the bow and examined it thoroughly—as when a man skilled in lyre-playing and in song effortlessly stretches a new string round the peg, fastening the twisted sheep-gut at either end—even so, without effort, did Odysseus string the great bow. Then he took it in his hand and tried the string: it sang out sweetly, like the voice of a swallow. The Suitors were greatly vexed, and the colour of all of them changed. Zeus thundered loudly, giving an omen, and noble much-enduring Odysseus rejoiced at the sign sent him by the son of Cronos of the crooked counsels. He took a swift arrow which lay by on the table, naked: the rest were within the hollow quiver, those arrows which soon the Achaeans would sample. He held it on his forearm and drew back string and notched arrow end, sitting in his chair as he was, and aiming straight before him he let the arrow fly, and of all the axes he missed not one handle tip: the arrow with heavy bronze point went through them all to the door. And Odysseus said to Telemachus: 'Your guest who sits in your house has not shamed you, Telemachus: I have not missed that mark, nor did I labour long to string the bow; my strength is still unchanged, not as the Suitors in contempt reproached me. Now it is time for a supper to be got ready for the Achaeans while it is light, and then for play, with song and lyre—they are the ornaments of the feast.'   (21.404–30)

What is emphasised here is the ease and smoothness with which the hero does what nobody else could do at all. The comparison with a singer who strings his lyre is not only vivid but also pregnant. Repeatedly Odysseus has been compared to a professional singer: Alcinous actually said to him that he 'told his tale like a singer, well and skilfully', and it holds the Phaeacians entranced; Eumaeus, too, gazed at him 'as a man gazes at a singer'. The singer glorifies his calling and his audience by comparing his performance to that of a great hero before the fabulous Phaeacians, but perhaps there is also the meaning that action and the song of action are in a way one—he who does the deeds is creating the song and hearing its resonance. Again the simile is simple and striking, one of many in the *Odyssey* drawn from skilled trades: the similes which accompany the action of blinding the Cyclops are the most remarkable instance.

As often at intense moments, the pace of action quickens, and the intervention of Zeus takes less than one whole line to narrate. The adjective 'naked' of the arrow comes, as so often in the Homeric poems, by itself at the beginning of a line, as for instance when Athena says to Zeus 'My heart is burning for the prudent Odysseus, *luckless one*, who is suffering far from home': as often, it is a heavy and pregnant epithet. One arrow is stripped for action, as in a moment Odysseus 'stripped off his rags' in a gesture which flung off his old beggarly identity: the same word is used—*gumnos*, the naked arrow—*gumnōthē*, he stripped. The verb used of the Suitors 'sampling' the arrows—*peirēsesthai*—was used twenty lines earlier of Odysseus 'trying' the bow, *peirōmenos*: that introduces a grim humour—the Suitors will 'try' it in a very different sense. The unruffled superiority which Odysseus expresses in taking his time over checking his bow, then stringing it without apparent exertion, is continued as he shoots sitting down and addresses Telemachus with darkly playful irony. The Suitors have long feasted with music: now for a feast of death, and then for a real celebration. There will in fact be music and dancing when the Suitors are dead, a ruse of Odysseus to conceal their killing. All the passages in the poem which bear on hospitality and its abuses, and on meals and gruesome scenes during meals—the killing of Agamemnon, the cannibalism of the Cyclops—are to be felt as active behind the last grisly scene which now commences.

REPEATED VERBS AND SIMILES

Some procedures which are natural to Homeric style are worth a word of comment. In general expression it is paratactic: that is, it proceeds by adding separate clauses and sentences rather than by such 'subordinate' connections as 'although' or 'after'. Thus Odysseus answers Eurymachus' challenge that he is a work-shy idler:

> Eurymachus, I wish there could be a contest in work between us—in the spring time, when days are long—in the hay, I would have a curved sickle, and you would have the same, that we might try our hand at work—fasting right up to the sunset, and hay were there in plenty: or if there were oxen to drive, those which are the best, tawny and big, both fed full on hay, oxen of the same age and power—their strength is not slight—and there were a day's measure of land, and the filth

> were yielding to the plough: then you would see me, if I
> would drive a straight furrow. (18.366-75)

It is noticeable how many independent elements with verbs
there are in this passage, which in English, or in later Greek,
would be broken up into subordinate clauses.

We can observe also a tendency to repeat an important
word, lingering on it. This is essentially, like parataxis, a device of unsophisticated speech, though Homer's use of it
may be far from naive. In a simple form we find things like
the description of Hermes arriving on Calypso's island. Her
cave was worth seeing:

> There even an immortal who came by would *marvel* at the
> sight and delight his mind. There stood the Messenger,
> Argus-slayer, and *marvelled*; and when he *had marvelled* at it
> all in his heart... (5.74-76)

There is a greater difference in the verb forms in Greek than
in English—*thēēsaito, thēeito, thēēsato*—but the repetition is
enjoyed for its own sake. A spectacular instance comes in
Book Nineteen. Odysseus, disguised, is talking to Penelope
about her husband, whom he claims to have entertained in
Crete, a false tale but like the truth:

> And as she listened her tears flowed and her flesh *melted* [or
> 'wasted', but we need this verb here]: as snow *melts* on the
> high hills, snow which the east wind *melts away* when the
> west wind has showered it down, and as it *melts* the rivers are
> brimmed full with it: even so did her fair cheeks *melt* as she
> shed tears, weeping for the husband who was sitting beside
> her. (19.204-209)

Forms of the verb *tēko* appear no less than five times in five
lines, and since the passage is a simile, a decorative poetical
device of a sophisticated kind, the explanation is clearly not
simple incapacity to think of another word. The resem-
blance between pining Penelope and melting snow is ham-
mered home by this device of loving repetition.

Extended similes are one of the glories of the Homeric
epic. To say 'he came like an eagle' or 'he raged like a bull'
is common to many poetic traditions: peculiar to Homer is
the elaborate comparison, which may run to eight or ten
lines. They are notably commoner in the *Iliad*, where they
multiply particularly in the scenes of killing in battle; not because the poet thinks such scenes are boring and wants to
liven them up, but from a desire to make these terrible
scenes as vivid as possible to the mind of the audience. The

Odyssey contains fewer passages of intense writing than the *Iliad*, but moments such as the blinding of the Cyclops or the stringing of the bow are underlined and made vivid by full-dress comparisons. Most of the similes in the *Iliad* are drawn from the fierce terrors of nature—storms, forest-fires, lions. When the *Odyssey* uses such material, which is seldom, a change can be seen. In the *Iliad* a lion attacks the cattle in the byre, 'and his haughty spirit drives him on': that simile is applied to a great Trojan hero attacking the Greek lines. In the *Odyssey* Odysseus, shipwrecked, naked, hungry, caked in brine, has to approach the princess Nausicaa and her maids to beg for help: 'He went on like a lion of the mountains, trusting in his strength, which goes through rain and wind . . . his belly drives him on'. The change from 'his haughty spirit' to 'his belly' is a significant one, conveying something of the different atmosphere of the two poems. Odysseus is always talking about his belly and its imperious demands: *that* is the sort of lion which he would resemble, hungry and bedraggled. . . .

HOMER'S PREFERENCE FOR DIRECT SPEECH

Nothing is more characteristic of Homer than the great amount of direct speech in the poems. Including Odysseus' narration of his own adventures, more than half the *Odyssey* is in direct speech. Like the narrative, speeches can vary greatly in tone and pace. Time stands still during the long stories told by Nestor and Menelaus, or during the false tales with which Odysseus amuses people on Ithaca ('I gazed at him as at a bard', says Eumaeus). Other dialogues can be positively laconic. For instance, two competing messengers come to tell Penelope of her son's return: one blurts it out in a single line, 'Your son is home, my queen'. Later in Book Sixteen we find guarded and curt speech. 'Let's tell *them* to come back', says Eurymachus, meaning their ambush party: no point in staying on now. But another Suitor has seen the ambush ship returning, and he says 'Let us not send a message: they are here. Either a god told them, or they saw the ship going past and could not catch it.' 'How the gods have got him out of trouble!' says Antinous bitterly. All these utterances are both short and also deliberately unrevealing. 'Them', 'they', 'him', 'the ship', are all things which must not be named out loud. Book Seventeen contains other conversations like this, which show that the formal manner ('the black ship of god-like Telemachus') is not the only one at the disposal of the *Odyssey*.

Indirect speech is not favoured by the poet. The seven lines in which Demodocus' song about Troy is reported are exceptional, caused by the poet's reluctance to go into details when what interests him is only the effect on Odysseus.... On the whole narrators are omniscient, telling us things which they could only have found out later, if at all, as if they were aware of them at the time. For instance Eumaeus, in the touching and lively story he tells of his being kidnapped by his nurse and a band of pirates when he was little—'a cunning little fellow, just trotting out of doors with me', the nurse calls him—reports for us all the details of the woman's assignation and conversation with the pirates, and when Odysseus goes up to a look-out he sees, not just smoke, but 'smoke from the house of Circe'. But there are moments when awareness is shown of this point. Hermes tells Calypso that she must let Odysseus go. She is forced to comply, but she tells Odysseus only that 'My mind is righteous, and my heart in my breast is not of iron: no, it is merciful'. Naturally Odysseus is astonished, and he never does find out why she did it: he tells the Phaeacians it was 'At a summons from Zeus, or else her own mind changed'. Calypso, very humanly, wants the credit for her enforced action. More remarkably, in Book Twelve Odysseus tells us of a conversation on Olympus between Zeus and the Sun-god. At the end of it he adds, 'This I heard from Calypso, and she said she heard it from Hermes the messenger'. This surprising touch shows a sudden twinge of conscience on the poet's part: how *did* Odysseus know all this? ...

Effects That Take on a Deeper Meaning

[Homer also used the device of irony in his poems.] The plot [of the *Odyssey*, for instance] involves a hero whose identity is unknown to many of the people among whom he moves: that was natural once he has returned incognito to Ithaca, but the scene among the Phaeacians need not have been developed in the same way, with Odysseus concealing his identity for hundreds of lines and only giving hints by his tears at Demodocus' Trojan songs, had not the poet positively enjoyed such effects.

They also are prominent in the first four books. Thus when Telemachus, encouraged by Athena in her disguise as

Mentes, tells the Suitors to get out of his house, Antinous replies, 'Telemachus, the gods themselves must be teaching you to speak up so boldly'. That is, as we know, truer than he thinks. At Pylos, Telemachus is seized with shyness about addressing the aged Nestor. Athena, again disguised, says to him, 'Telemachus, some things you will think of yourself, and others a god will put into your thoughts'. She means herself. In Pylos the newcomers are invited to join in a ceremony of prayers to Poseidon. Athena knows, and we know, that it really is Poseidon who is the obstacle to Odysseus' return, but to the other characters this special significance is unknown. So she prays: '"Hear us, Poseidon Earthshaker, and do not grudge us the fulfilment of these our prayers ..."' So she prayed, and she fulfilled it all herself'. We share her pleasure, and that of the poet, at seeing a meaning behind the surface of events.

When Odysseus is moving unrecognised in his own house, such effects take on a deeper meaning. Even the Suitors are aware, as they anxiously tell Antinous, that gods move disguised among men, in the shape of strangers, testing men for violence and good behaviour: suppose this beggar is a god? The poet derives special ironic effects from Odysseus' incognito, many things being said by him or in his presence which gain added meaning from knowledge of his identity. That goes furthest when Penelope is made to say to Eurycleia, 'Come, wash the feet of your master's contemporary'. The effect is much less unnatural in the Greek, and cannot be fully conveyed in English without overemphasis. In the context of recognition, the hint has a poignant quality. Odysseus allows himself several heavily ironical utterances, through which his true self peeps out. 'Be generous', he says to Antinous: 'I too was rich once and lived in a fine house'. Later he says that no labour will tire him, he will hold up the torches for the Suitors, 'Even if they decide to stay till morning they will not beat me: I am much-enduring'. We hear the allusion, lost on the Suitors, to his regular epithet, 'much-enduring Odysseus'; and 'they will not beat me' also looks forward, for us but not for them, to his battle with them. In the same vein is Penelope's first notice of the mysterious beggar. Perhaps he has seen or heard of Odysseus, 'for he is like a man of many travels'. Greek does not express 'a', and the line looks as if it could mean 'He is like the great traveller.' A last instance: when the bow is produced, the first of the Suitors to try and fail to draw it says

> My friends, I cannot draw it: let someone else take it. Many
> noblemen will this bow deprive of life and breath, since it is
> better to die than to live on and fail in our purpose.
>
> (21.152–54)

That speech, evidently designed for the sake of its ironic
opening, is truer than the speaker knows.

Homer's Use of Imagery, Symbols, and Formulas

Cedric H. Whitman

Anyone who reads Homer is immediately struck by his frequent use of formulas (or formulae), perhaps the most common literary device employed in oral poetry. In this context, a formula is a stock phrase or description that expresses a given idea and that is regularly repeated in the course of the narrative. Perhaps the most obvious examples in the *Iliad* and *Odyssey* are the many epithets, terms or phrases used to characterize persons or things, such as the "rosy-fingered Dawn," the "swift-footed Achilles," and the "far-darting Apollo." Homer also used formulas to express simple, often-repeated actions, such as sitting ("So speaking, he sat down") or initiating a speech ("He spoke these winged words"); or to describe physical conditions and appearances, such as that of mortally wounded warriors ("Night wrapped his eyes"). In this essay, Cedric H. Whitman, former professor of Greek at Harvard University and noted Homeric scholar, discusses how Homer employed formulas and other symbolic devices to create vivid mental images of the legendary heroic age depicted in his epic poems.

Modern criticism tends to find the essence of poetic speech in metaphor, and to regard the art of poetry as primarily imagistic, while the more external elements of the form, meter, rhyme, and even the other rhetorical figures, are purely secondary. If this view is true, a serious question arises about Greek poets, especially Homer: how to account for the power of a poet who has always been found so singularly lacking in metaphor? It has been estimated that there are only twenty-five real metaphors in the whole first book of the *Iliad*, which has six hundred and eleven lines. At the rate of one metaphor in each twenty-four-and-a-half lines, few poems would be effective. Either metaphor cannot be so central, or else Homer has been overestimated. But there is a third alternative, that Homer may be indeed more metaphoric than has been thought. The directness of Homer's language is striking, but it is very far from the directness of prose. If it lacks metaphor in the modern sense, it is nonetheless a tremendous imagistic texture, and metaphoric in the sense that all language is, in a way, metaphoric. In order to make clear what is meant, it will be necessary to explore the meaning of metaphor and of poetic speech in general. It must also be borne in mind that in Homer we are dealing with an oral, traditional style, and that the problem therefore differs somewhat from the problem as found in written literature. This is not to say that the poems do not exhibit many of the virtues found in written literature; they do. Even a purely literary approach reveals many of their profound vistas. But the question of metaphor well illustrates the limits of the method. In the Homeric epic we have to deal with something which established many of the literary assumptions of Western culture, but which in its oral, traditional origins was modally different from all subsequent poetry.

Even on the surface, Homer is by no means lacking in figurative language. The most evident kind is, of course, the great epic simile, rising like a prismatic inverted pyramid upon its one point of contact with the action. Metaphor occurs, though sparsely: when fighters fall, they "sleep the brazen sleep," or "night wraps their eyes." The Achaeans are subdued by the "scourge of Zeus." The somewhat mysterious "bridges of war" may be metaphor. . . . Homer is unique in the ability to call things by their right names—helmet, ship, or shield—and make them strike the ear as rich and strange. Thus what might be called the "first level" of the poems, the rational, factual level, has an intense beauty of its own, which perhaps partly explains Homer's appeal to children. In any case, it makes him the most sensuously vivid of all poets; whatever extended implications may exist, it is never necessary to grasp these before one can feel the poetic fire of a scene. The simplest statements of fact or action have a compact vitality and immediacy which put all naturalistic modes of realism to shame. For all his scarcity of the more familiar types of figurative imagery, except simile, Homer's lines are as sharply imagistic as it is possible to conceive; all is clear, pure, and detailed. What is the secret of such a poetic method, which seems to do without so many of the poetic modes of other literature . . . ? To answer the question, one must examine the components of the epic style itself, and see in what way it is related to the imagistic and symbolic procedures of poetry in general.

IMAGES AND SYMBOLS

It is not easy to find satisfactory definitions for the terms "symbol" and "image" as used in literary criticism. In general, however, the poetic symbol is a word or phrase which carries a larger meaning than that which it denotes, and this larger meaning is determined and limited by the contextual associations of the work in which it stands. . . . An image, on the other hand, is primarily a word or phrase devised to evoke sense impression, visual, auditory, or any other. Images may, and easily do, become symbols by association. . . . But the first function of an image is a direct appeal to that part of the mind which recognizes sense-experience. . . .

It is by means of the image and the poetic symbol, as defined above, that language is made presentational. Any word alone may be imagistic, except perhaps colorless modal auxiliaries, and any word may be a poetic symbol, hence presentational. But when a group of grammatically related words become presentational, it is because some technique has been employed to suppress their grammatical symbolism in favor of a presentational symbolism. The importance of the time element is consequently also diminished, since the sense of evolving thought is transcended by the imagistic unity of the total phrase. The techniques which so tend to identify groups of words with artistic rather than logical syntax are familiar: metaphor and the other figures, departure from colloquial order of words, actual omission of some grammatical factor which can easily be understood, meter with its effect of contrapuntally modifying the normal sound of words, rhyme which tends to emphasize sound over sense, and finally diction itself. For when we praise a poet's choice of a right or inevitable word, we must remember that it is chosen in reference to the poem's artistic end, and not for its dictionary meaning. Language thus used becomes imagistic and symbolic in a new sense. As a picture of a cat is a symbol of a cat, but not a definition of a cat, so too poetic language is a symbol of the thing represented, but not its definition. . . .

Any word, therefore, even the indefinite article, may become symbolic in a poetic scheme, that is, it may contribute presentationally and not merely grammatically to that scheme. Imagery does so in that its very diction, carefully selected, prompts a unified, though perhaps highly complex and articulated, sensory response. Symbols, in the full sense of poetic symbols, do so by virtue of their accumulated contextual meanings in the poem. To illustrate: in the first book of the *Iliad,* the image of fire occurs in the burning pyres of those dead of the plague. It is simply an image, and a vivid one. But in the course of the poem fire takes on a host of associations, and becomes in a sense the symbol of the chief action of the poem. Such a process is possible only in an art which employs a medium where meaning is both denotative and connotative. In spite, therefore, of the grammatical, discursive problem, words, with their specific denotative force and their power of almost infinite semantic expansion through connotation, offer perhaps the richest soil of all for artistic symbolism. Synonyms, for instance, by virtue of identical denotation, and even homonyms, or near-homonyms, through similarity of sound, may both contribute to the symbolic structure.

USING FORMULAS AS AN ART FORM

To return now to the *Iliad* and the *Odyssey*: it has sometimes been felt that the formulaic, oral style which Homer inherited from the epic tradition could not, since it was not his own creation, have anything to do with his genius, which was to be sought instead in his departures from oral method. But besides the fact that we cannot point to a single certain departure from the method, it must be said that Homer's genius is profoundly involved with the traditional style, and we shall not understand his unique power without first understanding the aesthetics of the style itself. . . .

One of the chief characteristics of the epic formula is that it regularly occupies a given metrical position in the hexameter [verse containing six measured feet, or beats, per line]. The proper name with its epithet is many times more frequent at the end of a line than at the beginning. The word "hand" is very frequent in the *Iliad*; in the nominative or accusative plural, if modified by "invincible," it invariably closes the line; but the phrase "in his hands" always begins the second foot of the hexameter. A glance at the Homeric concordance could multiply examples of such practice almost to infinity. A formula is, in fact, a semantic unit identified with a metrical demand, and it is a testimony to the extraordinary strictness and economy of the singers that there are so few duplications, or formulaic alternatives with the same meaning and metric. There are a very few exceptions, and certainly a word changes position more easily than a phrase does, but in general both words and phrases are fixed in definite metrical positions.

Another peculiarity of the epic formula is the semantic unity of its parts. This is especially true of noun-and-epithet combinations, such as "Agamemnon king of men," "swift-footed horses," and "rose-fingered dawn." These are not meant to be heard analytically, but more as names given in full; they are the equivalents of Agamemnon, horses, and dawn, and, often repeated, fall on the ear as units. Yet they are ornamental units also, and richer than the mere nouns alone would be. Furthermore, such unity is not confined to phrases involving nouns with epithets. The battle books of the *Iliad* abound with a bewildering variety of formulae, all metrically different, but all conveying the fall of a warrior who has his death wound: "his limbs were loosened," "he seized the earth with his palm," "night wrapped his eyes," "his armor rattled upon him" (as he fell), and a great many others. All frequently recur, and once their meaning is known, the ear no longer distinguishes the words so much as accepts the phrase whole. "So speaking, he sat down" crystallizes to a single image. Some formulae even fill whole lines, yet their essential unity is not lost: "Thus he spoke, and brandishing hurled a long-shadowing spear." One may break this down into words, but one tends to read it, or hear it, simply as one expression, embodying the act of ceasing to speak and hurling a long spear. The line is a unity, and even the strongly imagistic word "long-shadowing" does not dominate its force, which is kinetic and narrative. The mind's singularly unified response to the formula is observable in the beginning student's frequent ability to translate a formula correctly, though he may have forgotten which word means what. The process can extend even to those passages of many lines, such as the descriptions of a feast, launching a ship, or arming for battle. Such nonanalytic unity of meaning also is functional in origin. The singer wanted a phrase with a certain meaning and devised it; once devised, it could be reused, but only as a whole. To break it up or alter it was possible, but then one made another whole. The formula, not the word, was the epic unit. And the same is true of the longer repeated scenes. They might be lengthened or shortened, but they were units, to be used as such.

One might, therefore, describe the epic formula as an artificially devised unit of semantic, grammatical, and metrical functions. As such, it has clearly transcended the discursive function of speech, and has become a vividly presentational medium, in short, an art form. Whether or not a given formula embodies an actual metaphor, it is nevertheless always imagistic, and appeals directly to the senses. Its artificially devised union of metric and meaning subordinates its grammar and suppresses the time sense, so that from the materials of a discursive symbolism has been made a building block of a presentational symbolism. The formula is functional, therefore, not merely in the sense that it assists in creating verse, but also because it is a sort of poetic atom, a fragment of technically transformed speech whose structure is already that of art, not logic. . . .

Formulae That Keep Gaining Weight

On the other hand, since everything in the epic is formulaic, though highly varied formulaic speech, the functional aspect cannot in the large be the determining factor. Functions are functions of something, and in this case, of the poet's intention. The oral poet, like any other, must plan his lines, and he must have some notion of what the end will consist of when he sings the beginning. . . . The problem in oral composition was to . . . adjust the building blocks of the poetic speech with reference to association and design.

Another example of the use of a common formula in an uncommon way can be found in the *Patrocleia* [the section of the *Iliad* dealing with Patroclus's heroics and death], where Patroclus, attempting to scale the Trojan wall, confronts Apollo, and rushes at him, "equal to a god." The phrase is traditional enough, but here it takes on more than a merely honorific force. Patroclus is struggling with Apollo, and, as appears later, he is anything but Apollo's equal. Yet the poet has made it clear just before that Patroclus' great burst of courage is due to the direct inspiration of Zeus, and that this inspiration is yet a "calling unto death." The heroic association of divine valor with death involving a god is implied in the epithet, which moreover recalls Patroclus' first moment of involvement in the action which led to his death. This is the moment when, summoned by Achilles, he comes out of his tent "equal to Ares," and "it was the beginning of his woe." From here on till his death, Patroclus' epithets take on a divine context. One might multiply instances, but at the risk of seeming to isolate special moments of propriety, and obscuring the all-important fact of Homer's consistent felicity in the arrangement of formulae. Each one that seems singularly well chosen depends for its effect on hundreds of lines of texture which have prepared it. No one, for instance, can fail to notice the effect of the common phrase, "glorious gifts" which ends the *Patrocleia*, as the immortal horses of Achilles, "glorious gifts" from the gods to Peleus, carry the charioteer Automedon to safety, leaving Patroclus dead on the field. Its commonplace ring now takes on a peculiar irony, since all Achilles' glorious gifts hereafter will be vain and stale, mere commonplaces of his heroic position. Here it is almost impossible to draw the line between the poet and the style itself, yet the effect is there, an effect of terrible bitterness. Indeed, the whole line, unnecessary for the action alone, seems to have been added to emphasize the connection of Achilles with the Olympians who have espoused his cause and permitted the death of his friend. In Homer's scheme, instead of wearing themselves out, the formulae keep gaining symbolic weight, like rolling snowballs. Achilles is often compared to a lion, but when he strides out the door of his tent "like a lion" after threatening Priam, the image reflects in particular the helpless king's view of him; it cannot, in that moment, remain mere epic ornament. Even such a cliche as the rose-fingered Dawn, who mounts Olympus, passes from the functional to the symbolic by constant reference to the airy world of the gods . . . against which the deadly human drama is played. As one critic aptly remarked, everything becomes symbolic in the hands of a good poet. . . .

USE OF COMPLEX WEATHER SYMBOLISM

The relation between certain of Homer's scenes and the image contained in a formula is sometimes so close and ex-

plicit that some episodes seem to be scarcely more than formulae acted out like charades. In the fourth *Odyssey*
Menelaus relates how he was confined by adverse winds in
the island of Pharos for twenty days, until the sea nymph Ei-
dothea came to his rescue. He asks her which of the gods
"shackles and binds him from his path." The last two words
of the formula recur, with a slight change, in *Odyssey 5*,
where Athena stills the winds which have shipwrecked
Odysseus: "Then she bound the paths of the other winds."
The metaphor of being "bound" or prevented from a journey
by adverse winds, or, as in English, wind-bound, is reversed
into an image of binding the paths of the winds, which is the
function of a benign and favoring deity. So far, we meet here
only formulaic variations on a basic metaphor. But in Book
10 of the *Odyssey* the metaphor becomes action, a little scene:

> And he [Aeolus] stripped off the skin of a nine-years ox,
> Wherein he bound the paths of the blustering winds . . .
> And tied them in my hollow ship with a shining string
> Of silver, that not even a little might breathe through . . .

What was originally a figure of speech is acted out, with the
winds literally tied up in a bag with a silver string, which the
companions later undo, in one of their occasional moments
of insubordination. The episode comments eloquently on
the psychological interpretation of metaphor and magic, poetic speech and poetically conceived action.

Again, the description of Odysseus' landing in Phaeacia
and meeting with Nausicaa strikingly illustrates how a single formula with its image not only may underlie and mingle with the action, but also may externalize or objectify the
internal states of the characters and embrace a dramatic situation whole. After the struggles of the shipwreck, the hero,
exhausted, half-conscious, and vomiting brine, crawls
ashore at the river mouth, in a place free of stones, where
there was "a shelter from the wind." The passage is full of an
overwhelming sense of relief and salvation, but it arises not
from anything Odysseus says about it, but from the nature of
the things which he encounters. Of these—the land itself,
the slackened stream, the lack of stones—none is so central
to the feeling of benignity as the image of windlessness, the
cessation of all rough elements. The winds have had their
will in the shipwreck. One of the two things Odysseus still
fears now is that the wind will blow cold at dawn if he sleeps
on the shore; and he seeks the thicket of wild and domestic

olive, "Which neither the force of the damp-blowing winds / Pierced, nor the flashing sun struck with his rays, / Nor the rain poured through." There he falls asleep, like a spark hidden under ashes. This is logical enough, but it is also magical. A spark under ashes revives with wind, and presently there are winds; but with a subtle change. Homer is immersed in images of peace and safety, the focus of which is to be Nausicaa, herself an image of tender nurturing, peace, and every blessing of civilization. She cannot be a wind. At the beginning of Book 6, she is asleep, like Odysseus, but Athena, summoning her to his aid, comes into her safe chamber, through the closed doors, "like a breath of wind." This wind which rushes toward the bed of Nausicaa is a presaging token of the impact which the experienced, weather-beaten Odysseus is to have upon the sheltered Phaeacians, especially Nausicaa, an impact which is vividly dramatized in Book 8. This wind has action and danger in it, nicely imaged in the simile of the weather-beaten lion, when Odysseus comes out of the bushes toward the princess and tells her how wind and water brought him to Scheria. By contrast, Phaeacia, the land blessedly remote from all enemies, is a windless paradise: "Assist his bath," says Nausicaa to her friends, returning to the formula which keeps repeating itself, "where there is shelter from the wind." It is scarcely a wonder, in such an elaborate complexity of weather symbolism, that when Athena finally leaves Nausicaa in charge for the moment, she goes to an Olympus which, though it is much unlike the gods' dwelling as described elsewhere in Homer, is very like the safe thicket where Odysseus sleeps: "Neither by wind is it shaken, nor ever wet by rain, / Neither snow comes near it, but verily clear sky / Cloudless expands, and a white gleam spreads over all." It is a mistake to think that Homer has climbed in this vision of supernal tranquility to a nobler conception of the divine kingdom than he had in the *Iliad.* He is simply following the course of his imagery, and developing in action and description the vision which is most briefly caught in the formula, "where there was a shelter from the wind.". . .

The episodes just described, however, contain a great deal more than the images mentioned, and, of course, not every scene can be read backwards into a formula. The character of Nausicaa, for example, is a chef-d'oeuvre [masterpiece] quite apart from her symbolic function in the rescue of

Odysseus. Her own existence as a poetic creation, a paradigm of the day on which a girl becomes a woman, is an especially appealing example of the genius of the Greek artist for generalizing upon the individual without destroying individuality. But all Homer's characters are equally universalized individuals, and his scenes for the most part dramatize them for their own sakes, within the limits of a totally conceived heroic world. Thus, though the poetic image is the genesis of the dramatic or narrative scene, their dimensions and functions differ.

HIS WHOLE WORLD A METAPHOR

Yet many of Homer's scenes, apart from their relation to formulae, are just as traditional poetic units as the latter, and doubtless all are modeled to a degree on types. The battle books of the *Iliad* offer a dizzying variety of small combat scenes, whose recurrent motifs are combined and recombined into ever new situations, whose circumstances, like life itself, are always different, yet always coincide with others at certain points. It is a formal design corresponding to, but not specifically imitating, the natural world. Crystallized and formulaic, its life is not naturalistic but generic, its realism is classical, not that of photographic illusionism. The battle books, for instance, have been mistakenly neglected, for quite apart from their intimate connection with the whole structure, they better illustrate in one way Homer's skill with the oral style than do the more famous parts of the poem. Traditional as they are, Homer narrates them as images in a whole design. . . . When formulae are combined and recombined as they are in Homer's battle scenes, it is like the falling of glass chips in a kaleidoscope. Patterns constantly are formed, always with consistency of color, and always with pieces of the same shape, yet always different and always luminous with surprise. No matter how many are combined, the imagistic impact of formulae is not lost provided they are chosen with relevance to the total design which is aimed at. The poet's mind herein acts like the mirror in the kaleidoscope, constantly rounding the fall of formulae into an organic, larger unit.

The outlines of the larger units are, of course, determined by plot and character. . . . Thus the famous scene between Andromache and Hector has been finely analyzed as an interlocking of two main images, the world of man and the world of woman, which are hopelessly separate save for the unifying presence of a child. This is one view and an important one. But there are also many other ways of looking at it, for when an image is dramatized, it can never again be compressed; it exists in its own right as a scene, an image, but a kinetic one, an image of humanity in action.

But to speak of "images of humanity" leads to the most general considerations, and the question of Homer's ultimate intention as an artist. No mere analysis of the tools and technique of a poet can explain his power. The structural elements of epic, scene, simile, and formula subserve a total concept which in Homer's case is a vision of the heroic world of the past. Like all else Homeric, it is in part traditional, the keepsake of generations of bards, the long memory of the "glories of men." But it is also molded anew by each new hand for each new poem. It differs a little, though only a little, in the *Odyssey* from what it was in the *Iliad*, and hence it is always a creation, or a re-creation, never a mirrored imitation. It reflects nothing exactly, for it comes to being through the formulae which are . . . formalized units standing at a remove from reality in order to present it imagistically. It took centuries to forge this medium, and the pieces date from every generation of singers from the fall of Troy, or before, to the eighth century. Hence it arises that Homer's world is not the Mycenaean world, nor the world of the eighth century. It is the epic world, a visionary structure whose chief pillar is the heroic aspiration. Within that structure, all the elements fit, though they may not correspond precisely to anything outside it. . . . In Homer, every shield, even Ajax's big one, is the universal heroic shield, seen through centuries of admiring retrospect. It is "towerlike," or "equal all round," or "well turned" interchangeably, not because Homer forgot which kind of shield Ajax was carrying on a certain day, but because the only shield his Ajax ever had was an epic shield, symbolic of all that a heroic shield must be. It is a shield-metaphor, which changes with perfect unconcern from a Mycenaean body-shield to a round hoplite shield, reflecting any shape which had crept into the conventional speech by sometime being glorified in action. A completely plastic conception, the Homeric symbol, shield . . . is always a metaphor, and in Book XVIII of the *Iliad* it undergoes a tremendous expansion and becomes a metaphor of the whole heroic world. . . .

The answer to the problem of Homer's "directness," his apparent lack of metaphor, is now clear. His whole world is a metaphor, an enormously articulated symbolism of the heroic life. . . . Homer's metaphor . . . is in great part identical with the very language he speaks. For no matter how poor a singer used this speech, there is one virtue he could never lack, the momentary vividness of image after image. He might arrange his images badly, or repeat himself too often and in the wrong way, and thus dull the edge to a degree and fail of any real supremacy. But the epic medium was an extraordinary one, with some special advantages which, in the hands of a great singer, could lead to the *Iliad* and the *Odyssey*. Yet what was required of such a poet, in order to use the epic language to the full and create such poems, still, as in the case of all great artists, baffles analysis. The metaphoric world of the heroes which Homer created lay in fragments like the chips of stone and gold before a mosaic is made. The pieces were ideally suited to the purpose, but it remained to conceive the total design around a central theme, and then, within that design, to set all the formal building blocks in such a way that they would pick up light and shadow from each other in a consistent symbolic scheme. If the scheme is right, everything within it will be symbolic; but everything must be seen symbolically for the scheme to be right. At this point, we must leave it to Homer.

Homeric Honor and Cultural Values

J. Frank Papovich

Like other classical scholars who have attempted to teach Homer's epics to modern high school and college students, J. Frank Papovich of the University of Virginia has found that first-time readers of Homer are often disturbed by or confused about the strong preoccupation with war and warlike values displayed by many of the characters in the *Iliad* and *Odyssey*. In this essay, Papovich explains how he attempts to show his students that the value system of the society Homer depicted was very different than those of later cultures, including our own. For most people in Homeric society, he says, life revolved around the noble households of strong warrior chiefs and the kinsmen and followers under their protection; and war was a vital necessity for maintaining the social standing and honor of these rulers. It is essential to consider the unique cultural context of Homeric values, Papovich insists, "for if we fail to understand the original intentions in the Greek text, we may fail, in large part, to understand the text at all."

"With blood and muck all spattered upon him," Hektor leaves the battle raging on the plains of Troy and returns to the city, where he finds Andromache with their infant son at her breast. Together they speak of the horrors of war and the harsh specter of her enslavement by an Achaian warrior. Hektor reaches out to his son, who shrinks in fright from his dreadfully armed father. Then, in what seems a momentary respite from the terror of their world, Hektor removes his plume-crested helmet, tenderly jostles his now quieted son on his armed breast, and prays to the Olympians:

> Zeus, and you other immortals, grant that this
> boy, who is my son,

Reprinted by permission of the Modern Language Association of America from J. Frank Papovich, "Focusing on Homeric Values," in *Approaches to Teaching Homer's* Iliad *and* Odyssey, edited by Kostas Myrsiades; copyright ©1987 by the Modern Language Association of America.

may be as I am, preeminent among the
    Trojans,
great in strength, as I am, and rule strongly over
    Ilion;
and some day let them say of him: "He is better
    by far than his father,"
as he comes in from the fighting; and let him kill
    his enemy
and bring home the bloodied spoils, and delight
    the heart of his mother.
                              (*Il.* 6.476–81; trans. Lattimore)

Coming on this scene, many of our students may be disturbed by Hektor's prayer. After all, they reason, should not
such a father, troubled by the thought of his wife's grief,
wish that his son be spared the agony of war and pray instead for a life of peace?

As contradictory as this prayer may seem, other passages
are still more difficult to resolve. Throughout the *Odyssey*,
for example, students come to sympathize more and more
with Odysseus. Overcoming every obstacle of men and gods,
he longs only to return to the land of his father, his home,
and his wife and son. Yet the relief and joy that many students feel on Odysseus's return often vanish as his "blood-
thirsty" vengeance unravels. If our students see the climax of
the *Odyssey* as an unjustified slaughter of the suitors ... we
may be forced to allude to "the way things were" or to apol-
ogize for the "barbaric" excesses of our once honorable
hero. But by doing so, we risk leaving students with a bitter
aftertaste of what may be their first and last sampling of ancient Greek literature.

Before we accept such a situation, we should make every
effort to help students understand not only the texts before
them but also the cultural context that gave rise to such
texts. This endeavor is especially important in teaching the
Homeric texts, which, as oral narratives, are far more in-
debted to the traditions of their culture than are most literary narratives. Yet the need to inform ourselves of the cultural context of the Homeric poems is often unrecognized.
We are lulled into a false confidence by our perspective on
the ancient Greeks and their traditions. So much of their culture stands as a source of our own that we often assume that
these Greeks must have judged people and reacted to events
as we do. We need, however, to set aside our familiar per-
ceptual patterns and the misleading assumptions they gen-

erate. For if we fail to understand the original intentions in the Greek text, we may fail, in large part, to understand the text at all.

COMPETITION VERSUS COOPERATION

We can help our students better understand Homeric values by examining selected words from the original Greek texts. A rudimentary familiarity with the concerns of Homeric society, combined with close study of the range of key Greek value words in the texts, enables students to see beyond the patterns of their own culture and begin to understand the culture that informs the actions of the Homeric characters.

As an aid to our study of key Greek value words, lexicons are of limited help. By dividing up words, particularly value words with abstract connotations, into different "meanings," lexicons may fail to communicate why such words behave as they do. Consider, for example, the word *arete*, which has the various meanings of "goodness, excellence, prowess, success, prosperity, strength." It is more useful to think of value words as having a range of usage rather than many different meanings of which we must choose only one. . . .

When we translate *arete* as "good," we can assume that the evaluative meanings of the Greek and English are nearly the same—both words approve of the thing to which they are applied. Yet the qualities that determine "goodness" in things of the same kind may not be the same in Greek as in English. For example, the quality that most often characterized a man with *arete* was his success alone, with the means of his success counting for little or nothing. But in our culture, these means may indeed be more important in determining a person's goodness than the simple fact of success.

To discover what qualities were most important to Homeric man, we need to make one further distinction in evaluation. . . . In any society value words may be divided into two broad groups. The first . . . [termed] "competitive," refers to evaluations made on the basis of success or failure, with success ranked highest. Intentions are of no importance. We would not commend a general by saying he was a good commander but never won any battles. Success in war is paramount; intentions matter little, for no one intends to fail. Intentions do matter, however, with the second group of value words, which refer to cooperative activities. In cooperative arrangements, such as contracts or alliances, justice and fairness are of primary importance, and questions about intentions are appropriate. We might well want to know if a general is a good ally. Before deciding, we might ask if in his attempt to win a battle he intended to sacrifice the troops of his allies.

ALL-AROUND EXCELLENCE

In this excerpt from his noted study of Greek culture, The Greeks, *scholar H.D.F. Kitto offers this explanation of* arete, *an ancient Greek word and concept that cannot be easily or precisely translated.*

If [*arete*] is used, in a general context, of a man it will connote excellence in the ways in which a man can be excellent— morally, intellectually, physically, practically. Thus the hero of the *Odyssey* is a great fighter, a wily schemer, a ready speaker, a man of stout heart and broad wisdom who knows that he must endure without too much complaining what the gods send; and he can both build and sail a boat, drive a furrow as straight as anyone, beat a young braggart at throwing the discus, challenge the Phaeacian youth at boxing, wrestling or running; flay, skin, cut up and cook an ox, and be moved to tears by a song. He is in fact an excellent all-rounder; he has surpassing *arete*. So too has the hero of the older poem, Achilles—the most formidable of fighters, the swiftest of runners, and the noblest of soul; and Homer tells us, in one notable verse, how Achilles was educated. His father entrusted the lad to old Phoenix, and told Phoenix to train him to be 'A maker of speeches and a doer of deeds'. The Greek hero tried to combine in himself the virtues which our own heroic age divided between the knight and the churchman.

As students will discover in studying the conflicts between Achilleus and Agamemnon and between Odysseus and the suitors, the competitive values were more highly regarded than the cooperative. For in Homeric society, the balance between existence and annihilation was precarious. Cooperative virtues were valued, but in times of crisis, which were frequent, the preeminence of the competitive qualities and of the success they imparted became unmistakable. With such a scale of values, disputes between chiefs who were sufficiently angry to refuse arbitration could not be settled by referring to the "higher" virtues of cooperation, even in joint military expeditions. Further, since there was no authority higher than each individual chief and since concession to informal arbitration might have been regarded as a sign of weakness or failure, the seeds of dispute were inherent in the system. . . . Indeed, the main plots of both the Homeric poems reflect what occurs when such competition progresses from an abstract value to concrete action. . . .

WAR A BRUTAL NECESSITY

The social organization and value system of the Homeric poems are based firmly on the *oikos*, or the noble household, which was the highest form of political and economic as well as social organization. The *oikoi* were spread across the countryside with no other governing institutions to promote their growth and well-being or to prevent their complete annihilation. Some sense of community undeniably existed in Homeric society, but in a crisis, or whenever the aims of the *oikos* diverged from those of the wider community, the claims of the *oikos* were always primary.

Command of each *oikos* was the responsibility of the local warrior-chieftain who was both denoted and commended by the synonymous adjectives *agathos* and *esthlos*. Given the autonomy of the *oikos* and the absence of any higher authority, preserving the *oikos* clearly required the martial abilities of the *agathos*, whose qualities were denoted and commended by the noun *arete* (superlative adjective form: *aristos*). *Arete* was the power or ability to succeed in some action, and the highest use of *arete* commended the successful warrior, the *agathos*. To help students discover this emphasis on success in war, I ask them to consider the following short passage, an address of the Lykian Sarpedon to his comrade Glaukos:

> Glaukos, why is it you and I are *timan*, honoured,
> before others
> with pride of place, the choice meats and the
> filled wine cups
> in Lykia, and all men look on us as if we were
> immortals,
> and we are appointed a great piece of land by the
> banks of Xanthos,
> good land, orchard and vineyard, and ploughland
> for the planting of wheat?
> Therefore it is our duty in the forefront of the
> Lykians
> to take our stand, and bear our part of the
> blazing of battle,

so that a man of the close-armoured Lykians may
  say of us:
"Indeed, these are no ignoble men who are lords
  of Lykia,
these kings of ours, who feed upon the fat sheep
  appointed
and drink the exquisite sweet wine, since indeed
  there is *esthlos*, strength
of valour, in them. . . ."   (*Il.* 12.310–21)

With only two key words transliterated, my students can
better see the values that motivate these warriors to join
gladly "in the blazing of battle." Sarpedon and Glaukos de-
serve the position of *agathos* because they fight in the first
ranks, and there they either succeed and win honor or die and
bring honor to their opponent. What becomes clear, then, is
that the *agathoi*, originally a response to warlike conditions,
came to value and even need war as a means of maintaining
privileged status. A brutal necessity, war grew to have a positive value for the *agathoi*. And so Hektor's puzzling wish for
his son's happiness in a life of war and bloodied spoils becomes much easier for our students both to understand and
to justify. If Astyanax, son of Hektor and Andromache, were to
lead the best of lives, war was necessary.

TIME, KINSMEN, AND GUEST-FRIENDS

Another important concept closely associated with *arete* is
time. *Time* is usually rendered "honor," "compensation," or
"penalty"—a combination, as we see it, of dissimilar elements. Verb forms are *tinein* and *timan*, rendered "to
honor"; (*apo*) *tinein*, "to pay a price"; and (*apo*)*tinesthai*, "to
punish." While often denoting and chiefly acquired by the
possession of material goods, *time* is not equivalent to such
goods. A man's *time* is his position on a scale that ranks gods
at the top and the homeless beggar, such as the disguised
Odysseus on his return to Ithaka, at the bottom. To honor
(*timan*) a man is to move him away from the position of de-
fenseless beggar. To dishonor (*atiman*) a man is to do the re-
verse. Thus *time* denotes and commends all that distinguishes the life of a prosperous *agathos* from that of a
beggar—property, rights, and status.

Time was not an absolute quality but, rather, a relative
quality (available in limited quantity). *Time* awarded to one
man must be *time* withdrawn from another. To get back *time*
is *tinesthai*, "to punish." But translating *tinesthai* "to punish"

is not always appropriate. While the sack of Troy was *tinesthai* in the sense of "to punish," that punishment also and more fundamentally involved getting back *time* in the form of Helen, the goods stolen from Menelaos by Paris, the stripped armor of the Trojan warriors, and the booty acquired in the general looting of the city. . . .

While each *agathos* was well prepared to defend his *time* and *oikos*, no *agathos* could depend on himself alone. And since human beings in Homeric society had no rights except those they could defend by force or have guaranteed by being members of an *oikos*, the family, retainers, and servants of the *agathos* who depended on his *time* in the form of food, clothing, shelter, and status could, in turn, be depended on by the *agathos*. The *agathos* and his dependents, thus constituting a tightly bound support system, were distinguished from the rest of the world by the word *philos* [kinsman-friend].

The *agathos* traveling away from his *oikos* presented a special problem, for outside the *oikos* there was no real central institution to protect the rights, much less the existence, of the traveler. The traveler must supplicate an *agathos* who headed an *oikos* and hope to be received as a *philos*. Such a dependent relationship between a traveler and an *agathos* was a type of *philos* relation denoted by the word *xeinos*, usually rendered guest-friend (*xeinos* can denote both guest and friend). Thus the stranger who had a xeinos had an effective substitute for a kinsman, a substitute who would defend his guest-friend as he would any other member of his *oikos* and who would react to a loss of *time* by his *xeinos* as a loss of his own *time*. The *agathos* who agreed to receive a suppliant had, in turn, imposed a similar set of obligations on the received traveler, in effect guaranteeing his own *time* should he ever travel to the homeland of his *xeinos*. (This explains why *xeinos* has the dual denotation of guest and host, for by accepting the rights of a guest, an *agathos* also accepts the responsibility of a host should the occasion arise.) These reciprocal obligations were typically observed by the exchange of *xeinos* gifts, denoted by the word *xeineia*. Never were such gifts given by a host without proper recompense, whether immediate or years away, to self or kin.

The meeting of the Lykian Glaukos and the Greek Diomedes provides an excellent example for students to see the power of the *xeinos* relationship. The two have met in the heat of battle, and Diomedes has asked who his opponent is. After detailing his Lykian ancestors, Glaukos is interrupted by a "gladdened" Diomedes:

> [Diomedes] drove his spear deep into the
>   prospering earth, and in winning
> words of friendliness he spoke to the shepherd of
>   the people:
> "See now, you are my *xeinos*, guest-friend, from
>   far in the time of our fathers.
> Brilliant Oineus once was *xeinos*, host, to
>   Bellerophontes
> the blameless, in his halls, and twenty days he
>   detained him,
> and these two gave to each other fine *xeineia*,
>   gifts in token of friendship.
>
> .   .   .   .
>
>   Therefore I am your *xeinos*,
>   friend and host, in the heart of Argos;
> you are mine in Lykia, when I come to your
>   country.
> Let us avoid each other's spears, even in close
>   fighting.
>
> .   .   .   .
>
> But let us exchange our armour, so that these
>   others may know
> how we claim to be *xeinoi*, guests and friends,
>   from the days of our fathers."   (*Il.* 6.214–31)

Without understanding the situation of the traveler in Homeric society and the workings of the *xeinos* relationship, students usually view this exchange as little more than a quaint aberration in the mechanics of Homeric warfare. But having gained even slight familiarity with Homeric culture, students can see the sense of this pause in battle. While neither Glaukos nor Diomedes have seen or perhaps even heard of each other before, they are *philos* and *xeinos* to each other because of their grandfathers' *xeinos* relationship. Such *xeinos* bonds, furnishing Homeric society with what little stability it possessed, could not be canceled by something so fleeting as a ten-year war between "countries." Diomedes is more closely bound to Glaukos than he is to those Achaians who are not *philos* or *xeinos* to him.

ODYSSEUS'S VENGEANCE JUSTIFIED

The vengeance of Odysseus, so apparently excessive if students judge by modern-day standards, becomes easier to understand and to justify in the light of such elementary knowledge of Homeric values. Students can weigh the seriousness of the suitors' crimes against Odysseus by noting his yearning for return. He bases his desire for homecoming not simply on his love for Penelope or his longing to see his now grown son, Telemachos (strong as such emotions may be), but more fundamentally on his desire to return to *oikos* and *philoi*. As Odysseus himself claims in refusing Kalypso's invitation: "But even so, what I want and all my days I pine for / is to go back to my *oikos*, house, and see my day of homecoming." That this should be Odysseus's response wholly befits a man in a society where the necessities of self-preservation and satisfaction are inextricably bound up within the *oikos*. Students can perceive the suitors' offenses as threats to Odysseus's *oikos* and to the continued existence of himself and his *philoi*. Along with the accompanying loss of *time*, such a threat, most obvious in the squandering of the food and wine of the *oikos* and in the open abuse of Telemachos and Penelope, demands a response from Odysseus.

Alerted to the importance of *time* and the *xeinos* relationship, students can understand why the suitors' repeated insults to suppliants aggravate the seriousness of their crimes and justify the vengeance of Odysseus. For not only has his food been wasted in his absence, but when he appears at his own hearth to beg for what is rightfully his, it is denied him by men who squander it before his eyes. The suitors' mockery of Odysseus's supplications only increases the depravity of their offenses. . . . By cataloging the suitors' accumulated offenses against the *time* of Odysseus, most students who are initially troubled by Odysseus's vengeance come to see that the offenses against him are so great that the code of the *agathoi* binds him to refuse the gifts offered by the suitors (an act paralleled by Achilleus's refusal of Agamemnon's gifts) and to extract full recompense—*tinesthai*—by killing them all.

Given the central importance of *arete*, a wronged *agathos* naturally set the highest priority on obtaining recompense and restoring his *arete* even if by violence. This cultural truth provides students with the key not only to Odysseus's vengeance but also to Achilleus's wrath. For if the other Greeks cannot convince either Odysseus or Achilleus to cooperate, their claim to act as they please in restoring their honor is stronger than any other claim.

To view the Homeric poems from such a perspective allows our students to experience important and often neglected aspects of these oral epics. . . . We need not let our students forget that what we see of human beings in Homer is, in essence, little different from what we see today. Patterns shift and change, but much that is fundamentally human remains. And, indeed, the tragic moral of the *Iliad* suggests that love, honor, pride, and above all the awareness of human mortality, though enmeshed in unique cultural forms, are as recognizable across the centuries as they were across the battle lines on the plains of Troy.

Homer's View of the Gods and Divinity

Walter F. Otto

In the following essay, Walter F. Otto, a German religion scholar and author of *The Homeric Gods*, makes the point that Homer's depiction of the Greek gods represents religious views that had evolved over the long span of Bronze Age Mycenaean times and the Greek dark age that followed the collapse of Mycenaean civilization. Along the way, Otto explains, the Greeks borrowed deities and religious concepts from eastern peoples such as the Babylonians and Phoenicians; yet in incorporating these alien religious elements, the early Greeks reshaped them to their purposes and made them uniquely Greek in spirit. In his epic poems, Homer immortalized this new picture of the divine, in which the gods were seen as being one with nature and willing to intervene directly in human affairs.

The Homeric poems are based upon a clear and unified view of the world. They give evidence of this view at almost every verse, for every significant thing they say is associated with it and through this association receives its peculiar character. Remote as this view of the world may be from what other peoples and ages regard as religion, we call it religious nevertheless, because for it the divine is the fundamental basis of all being and happening, and this basis shines so clearly through all things and events that the Greeks themselves must needs speak of it in connection with even the most ordinary and familiar matters. For them no part of life is wholly without the divine.

Lofty Spirit and Noble Content

The religious outlook of the Homeric poems is clear and self-contained. . . . It can be collected methodically and accu-

Excerpted from Walter Otto, *The Homeric Gods*, translated by Moses Hadas (New York: Random House, 1954). Reprinted by permission of Thames & Hudson Ltd., London.

rately, sifted and listed, and it yields specific answers to questions of life and death, man and god, freedom and fate. Unmistakably a criterion for the nature of the divine emerges. The images of individual divine personages are also firmly delineated. Each of them possesses its special character, clearly defined in all its traits. The poet can assume that the listener has a vivid idea of the being and essence of every god. Whenever he introduces a god he characterizes him in a few strokes; these are always set down with the mastery which for millennia has been admired in Homer but which has not generally been recognized in scenes where gods figure. Yet it is just such scenes that must have given perceptive audiences special pleasure by their aptness. But for us the few strokes by which the god is vividly presented to our eyes are a precious index to his essence, and from all such strokes taken together his complete figure is articulated.

The divine, presented with such clarity in the Homeric poems, is manifold in form and yet everywhere consistent. A lofty spirit, a noble content, is expressed in all of its forms. It is not the purpose of the poems to communicate any religious revelation, to give force to any religious doctrine. They desire only to behold, and in the joy of beholding to fashion forms; before them lie all the riches of the world, earth and heaven, water and air, trees, animals, men and gods.

The view of the world which speaks out of these poems breathes a spirit which we must call specifically Greek. We may not overlook the fact that succeeding ages produced many views and aspirations of a quite different orientation. But if we observe the large and decisive lines of Greek genius we cannot doubt that it is the Homeric direction that they followed. The Homeric mode of seeing and thinking is continued, despite all temporal and individual variations, in the representative works of Greek genius, whether in poetry, plastic art, or philosophy. It possesses all the marks of what we call Greek, in contradistinction to other species of humanity, especially the oriental [eastern]; and it possesses this character as a thing natural and obvious. Its world view and its mode of thought must therefore have made their appearance in the centuries before the completion of the Homeric epics. For the spiritual process that then transpired we unfortunately have no direct evidence; only the end result stands before us in its power. Nor can we determine the duration of the epoch in question. Tempting as it may seem to bring the change and transformation of thought into connection with the succession of cultural eras, such as the Mycenaean and post-Mycenaean, we must abstain from any such attempt because we do not possess the necessary documentation. But even though the historical course must remain dark, the development of the spiritual process is clear and plain. The Homeric poems exhibit the new view of the world, which is decisive for Hellenism, in its mature and fixed form. And there are enough remains and echoes, not least in Homer himself, from which we may formulate some notion of earlier thought and belief.

DEITIES OF EARTH AND DEATH

The old faith was earth-bound and as much constricted by the elemental as ancient existence itself. Earth, procreation, blood, and death are the great realities which dominated it. Each of these had its own sacred sphere of images and needs, and the rigor of their here and now could be abated by no freedom of reason. Kindly and benevolent to those who remained loyal to them, terrible to any who—whether out of willfulness or necessity—disregarded them, they enclosed the life of the community and of the individual by their unalterable ordinances. They are a multiplicity but belong to the same realm, and they are not only related to one another but all flow together into a single large essence. This we can see in the divinities in which they are represented: all belong to the earth, all have a share in life as in death; whatever their individual traits may be, all may be designated as deities of earth and of death.

This marks the sharpest of distinctions from the new gods, who belong neither to the earth nor to the elemental in general and have no dealings with death. But the ancient world of gods was not forgotten even in later times and never wholly lost its power and its sanctity. The Olympian religion displaced it from its primacy, but it allowed it to subsist in the background, with that magnanimous liberality and truth which distinguish it. Greek faith underwent no dogmatic revolution, as did the Israelite or Persian, which reduced the older worship to superstition or rebelliousness against the sole domination of the new lord. Even in Homer, the purest witness to the Olympian religion, the elemental retains its ancient character of sanctity, and the divine spirits which derive from it come forward meaningfully at their appropriate times. We are therefore still able to obtain a reasonably precise picture of the nature of the ancient world of gods. . . .

ATHENA

Worship of Athena can apparently be traced back to the early period. Her name itself points to a source outside the Greek range, to which neither its root syllable nor its word-form can belong.

The likeness of an armed goddess with body almost wholly covered by a shield occurs frequently in Mycenean art. A familiar painted stucco relief from Mycenae shows this goddess, almost wholly hidden by her huge shield, at the center, with two women worshipping her at right and left. It has been believed that this figure represents the Mycenean Athena, and no one can deny the plausibility of this interpretation. But this tells us very little about the early history of our goddess; Cretan and Mycenean statuary is for us, unfortunately, virtually mute. We see a goddess covered by her shield, ready to attack or to guard. But is this all that her figure suggested when belief in her was a living thing? Should we call her maiden of the shield, maiden of battles? We are given no answer to this question. For the Homeric Athena, at least, such designations are not appropriate, joyous and mighty in battle as the goddess may appear. She is much more than a goddess of battle; she is, in fact, the sworn enemy of the wild spirit whose sole delight is the rush of combat. First of all we are inclined to think of the so-called Palladium and the many famous statues of armed Athena, although we are aware that the city of Athens, which bore the goddess's name, worshipped in the old temple on the Acropolis a carved wooden image which was not of this type. The ancient heroic legend in which Athena is so much involved exhibits her as a goddess of vigorous but by no means exclusively military action. Very few of the deeds of [the legendary hero] Heracles, at which her presence was an inspiration and a help, were of such a sort that his divine patroness could be called the maiden of battles. She does stand by Achilles, Diomedes, and others of her favorites in battle, but she also helps Jason build his ship and Bellerophon tame his horse. She stands at Odysseus' side in all manner of difficult situations. None of these operations can be assigned, unless by sheer caprice, to an earlier stage in the development of belief in Athena. If we do so assign them, we disrupt the unity of the Homeric and post-Homeric picture of Athena even before we have attempted to understand it. But it is very easy to understand if we do not, out of stubborn insistence on seeing a product of accident, close our eyes to the consistent and meaningful entity. . . .

APHRODITE

"Golden" Aphrodite, goddess of love, bears a name certainly not Greek. We know that she came to Greece from the east, but she was not only naturalized in pre-Homeric times but became wholly Greek. She was the great goddess of fertility and love of the Babylonians, Phoenicians, and other Asiatics, and is mentioned in the Old Testament as "queen of heaven." Definite word of her immigration survives. According to [fifth-century B.C. Greek historian] Herodotus the mother sanctuary was that of Aphrodite Urania at Askalon [a town in ancient Palestine]; it was thence, as he says, that the Cyprians themselves derived their cult of Aphrodite. . . . The *Odyssey* speaks of her sanctuary in Paphos on Cyprus. The name Cytherea, used in the *Odyssey* and later very famous, recalls the island Cythera. It was thither, according to [seventh-century Greek writer] Hesiod's *Theogony*, that the goddess went directly she arose from the sea, and it was from there that she first came to Cyprus. . . .

But we can leave the question of historical origins open without fear that we shall miss data essential for understanding the Greek goddess. Whatever the Orient or prehistoric Greece may have contributed to her image, its basic character is thoroughly Greek. The idea which the name Aphrodite denotes for us is a genuine expression of the spirit of pre-Homeric Hellenism, and we need direct our attention only to that idea. Through it even traits whose oriental origin is unmistakable acquire a new aspect and a particular sense. . . .

HERMES

Hermes, "the friendliest of the gods to men," is a genuine Olympian. His essence possesses the freedom, the breadth, and the brilliance by which we recognize the realm of Zeus. And yet he has properties which set him apart from the circle of the children of Zeus and which, when they are closely examined, appear to belong to a different and older conception of deity.

If we compare Hermes with his brother Apollo or with Athena we notice a certain lack of dignity in him. This appears quite plainly in the Homeric narrative whenever Hermes comes to the fore. His function as messenger of the gods is first mentioned in the *Odyssey*, and not in the *Iliad*, but we sense that this role suits his character perfectly. For his strength lies in resourcefulness. His works do not so much exhibit energy or wisdom as nimbleness and subtle cunning. . . . When the gods wished to put a stop to Achilles' cruel abuse of the body of Hector, their first thought was to have Hermes steal it. He distinguished his son Autolycus among all men in the accomplishments of thieving and perjury, which he himself possessed to such a high degree. Hence favorite epithets for him are "crafty," "deceiving," "ingenious," and he is the patron of robbers and thieves and all who are expert in gaining advantage through trickery. But his wonderful deftness makes him the ideal and patron of servants also. All that is expected of a diligent servant—skill in lighting the fire, splitting kindling wood, roasting and carving meat, pouring wine—comes from Hermes, whose qualities made him so efficient a servant to the Olympians.

Admittedly, these are no dignified arts, even if, according to the ancient Greek view, a hero is free to avail himself of them on occasion. But the lifelike total picture which Homer presents, whenever he has Hermes appear in person, speaks more clearly than do scattered indications of his character. In that picture we see the gay master of happy chance, never at a loss, who is little troubled by standards of pride and dignity, but who despite all remains lovable: genius in bringing men luck would be pointless if it could not win affection. In the battle of the gods in the twenty-first book of the *Iliad* our rogue supplies the conclusion. After Ares and Athena have had their tiff and Apollo, with stately dignity, has refused to do battle with Poseidon, and after the typically feminine scene between Hera and Artemis which follows as a postlude, Hermes declares to Leto, with a joking reference to the treatment which Artemis would receive at Hera's hands, that he has no intention of fighting with her and would care not at all if she would boast among the immortal gods that she had vanquished him by might and main. In the account of the love of Ares and Aphrodite, Apollo and Hermes are present as spectators, and Apollo asks his brother, with comic solemnity, whether he would not choose even the bondage of chains if so he might share Aphrodite's bed. Then, with the same comic dignity with which the question was put, the ingenious contriver of good luck answers that even if there were thrice as many chains, and all the gods and goddesses to look on, he would still be happy to languish in the arms of golden Aphrodite. The Apollo whom the poet here presents us is big enough not to play schoolmaster to his rascal of a brother, and is even amused by him. And so are we, if we are capable of appreciating the spirited gaiety, by no means frivolous, with which the witty poet has informed his tale. But however much this Hermes may amuse us, his character, as we have seen, marks him as strikingly different from all the other great Olympians. . . .

HERMES AND PRIMITIVE MAGIC

[This] brings us to the aspect of magic in his behavior. Magic played no inconsiderable part in the prehistoric world-outlook, but in Homer, except for a few traces, it has been left behind. Almost all of it that remains is attached to the figure of Hermes, whose position as arch-wizard and patron of magic is of long standing. In the *Odyssey* he shows Odysseus the magic herb that would counteract the enchantment of Circe. He possesses a magic wand with which he puts men asleep and awakens them. Just as he himself makes himself invisible at will by means of the cap of Hades, so his son Autolycus has the miraculous gift of changing things and making them unrecognizable. His whole character and presence stand under the sign of magic, though magic too, as we shall soon see, received a new and more spiritual meaning in the Olympian world.

The primitive element in Hermes is revealed by his very name, which points to cult usages of high antiquity. His pillar stood upon a heap of stones by the wayside, to which every passer-by piously added one. This gave him his name, for there can be no doubt that Hermes means "he of the stone heap." In later times the phallus [penis] remained as a characteristic of the stone pillars of Hermes, and this too points to a very ancient conception. The power of procreation . . . is by no means basic to Hermes' character. But we know of the phallic form in the sphere of the Titanic divinities, where it denotes a very massive aspect of primal ideology.

It appears, then, that the figure of Hermes can be traced

far back to an age whose habits of thought and perception were overcome by the new spirit. But there is a great chasm indeed between what we surmise of the ancient figure and the Homeric Hermes with his brilliance and inexhaustible abundance. . . .

NATURAL TRUTH VERSUS SUPERNATURAL MIRACLE

It is in the most astonishing images of divine manifestations, then, that we can most plainly see how alien to the spirit of true Greek piety is [the concept of a] miracle in the commonly accepted sense, which other religions seek out and sanctify. That piety is the more significant in that the same spirit accomplishes all things, from the greatest to the least, through the gods, indeed conceives of them as being accomplished by the gods themselves; and it is so completely alive to this relationship that it never forgets to emphasize the role of the divine even when the prowess of the most admired heroes is to be celebrated. . . .

In the epic, to be sure, where mighty men do and suffer, it is the extraordinary that is repeatedly brought before our eyes. But everywhere it presents itself in the same sense: not as the miracle of a god triumphing over nature, but rather as the experience of a great heart to whom—and to whom alone—at the height of his being and doing the deity presented itself out of the ordinary lines of nature.

In the face of this not much should be made of the circumstance that once in the *Iliad* the sun—that is, the sun-god—is made to set prematurely. The occasion is important enough. After a desperate struggle the Greeks finally succeeded in securing the corpse of Patroclus from the enemy. "They laid him on a litter, his comrades stood mourning around him, and among them fleet Achilles wept bitterly as he saw his true comrade lying dead upon his bier." Then, constrained by Hera, the sun set, "loth though he was," and all was quiet on the battlefield.—On a no less important occasion in the *Odyssey* Athena restrains the goddess Dawn and makes the night last longer. It was the night on which Penelope recognized her returned husband, and could not sate her eyes with gazing at him or loose her arms from around his neck. Now his wanderings and her lonely tears were ended. But these are isolated ventures of the poet, and in them everyone feels the natural truth which is the basis for their enduring effectiveness. They show an hour of life in its fateful grandeur, and it is that which grips us, not the absolute power of a god.

ATHENA HOLDS THE DAWN
In this passage from the Odyssey *the goddess Athena lengthens the night so that Odysseus and Penelope can better enjoy their first night together in twenty years.*

Penelope's surrender melted Odysseus' heart, and he wept as he held his dear wife in his arms, so loyal and so true. Sweet moment too for her, sweet as the sight of land to sailors struggling in the sea, when the Sea-god by dint of wind and wave has wrecked their gallant ship. What happiness for the few swimmers that have fought their way through the white surf to the shore, when, caked with brine but safe and sound, they tread on solid earth! If that is bliss, what bliss it was for her to see her husband once again! She kept her white arms round his neck and never quite let go. Dawn with her roses would have caught them at their tears, had not Athene of the flashing eyes bestirred herself on their behalf. She held the long night lingering in the West, and in the East at Ocean's Stream she kept Dawn waiting by her golden throne and would not let her yoke the nimble steeds who bring us light, Lampus and Phaethon, the colts that draw the chariot of Day.

Once the *Iliad* tells of a miraculous deed of Apollo. But the intensity of passion, which is given a lofty background in this picture, is unmistakable. The Trojan masses were streaming into the naval encampment. Dike, moat, or wall could not stop the furious chariots. It is Apollo who goes before them. The brandishing of his aegis threw the Greeks into such terror that they fled in panic. At the attack on the trench and wall "Apollo went before and kicked down the banks of the deep trench into its middle so as to make a great broad bridge. . . . He kicked down the wall of the Achaeans as easily as a child playing on the seashore kicks down the house of sand which he has built." At the beginning of this description it is expressly stated that the god was invisible.

ONE WITH THE DIVINE AND ETERNAL

As against the overwhelming impression of an abundance of evidence a few petty divergences signify little. The epic makes its conception of divine rule perfectly plain. The images which we have to learn from are indeed creations of the poet, but it would be myopic to see in them only the thoughts of an individual or small group. In contrast to what must have been the views of the earlier period, they give expression to a revolution in thought whose importance cannot be rated too high and which must necessarily have been consummated before poetry of the Homeric sort could be possible. For the more astonishing the specific character of Homeric faith must appear to us upon close examination, the more noteworthy is the fact that it presents itself with no pathos and no criticism or justification, as something natural and self-evident. Here there speaks a new race, grown perfectly sure of its conception of the world, calmly able to permit ancient and antiquated elements—and Homer knows a great many that were once important—to come forward out of the background as fairy-tales, without troubling about the alien spirit of these stories, which is perceptible even to us. And if any proof is still called for to show that what we have here are not merely the poet's fancies but Greek thoughts upon the world, the attitude of the Greek spirit in the post-Homeric age must carry conviction. For what is this attitude other than the acknowledgement of a nature which is not opposed to the divine and eternal but one with it? The extraordinary influence of Homeric epic upon Greek thought and creativity has often enough been stressed. It could not have become a guide to the future if it were not the expression of the true Greek spirit. Emerging victorious out of primeval visions, it here created its first and eternal monument.

Homer's Attitude Toward Death

Seth L. Schein

Seth L. Schein, a Homeric scholar who teaches at the University of California at Santa Cruz, suggests that Homer's portrayal of death, especially on the battlefield, is consistently straightforward and unsentimental. In this view, death is a natural end of life, at least for mortals—the gods who appear throughout the narratives of the *Iliad* and *Odyssey* can only be wounded, not killed. As Schein points out, Homer describes the brevity of the Trojan hero Simoeisios's life as unfortunate, less to create sympathy for him than to underscore that war, while in one sense glorious, has real human costs.

The Homeric attitude toward death is especially clear in the descriptions of the fates of numerous minor warriors, the little heroes who exist merely to be killed, whose deaths are the occasions for brief remarks or vignettes about their lives and manner of dying. As [Homeric scholar] Jasper Griffin has demonstrated, these "lesser heroes are shown in all the pathos of their death, the change from the brightness of life to a dark and meaningless existence, the grief of their friends and families. . . ." Certain motifs recur in their "obituaries": a man's life was brief; he died far from home and family; his comrades or parents or wife and children were bereaved; they were unable to help him and could not make good his loss. When the husband or son is young or newly married, the description of the death is especially moving; when emphasis is placed on the victim's ignorance of what was in store for him, or on his beauty and potential cut short, we are even more affected. Clearly, many of these motifs were traditional, but they are integrated with important themes of the *Iliad* itself. For example, as Griffin points out,

"The bereaved father is a dominant figure in the plot from Chryses to Priam, who appeals to Achilles in the name of another tragic father, Peleus." And all the young warriors who fall far from their parents and wives, whose comrades can do nothing for them, who die even as their ignorance of destiny becomes certain knowledge, culminate in Hektor. The descriptions of the deaths of the minor heroes help to create by their content and tone the consistent, unsentimental view of death and of life, that we think of as Homeric. They help us to interpret the overall dramatic situation and main story of the poem in a particular way. Homer never lets us forget that the minor warriors really are minor compared with the greater heroes who kill them, but the pathos he endows their deaths with makes us see what is lost in the glory of these greater heroes.

THE COST OF HEROIC ACHIEVEMENT

One passage that well illustrates Homer's attitude toward death is the description of the death of the Trojan warrior Simoeisios. This is one of the richest and most exquisite of many passages that recapitulate a central theme of the *Iliad*: the cost in human terms of heroic achievement. The death of the Trojan youth is analogous on a small scale to the death of Hektor and the destiny of Troy as they are portrayed and prefigured elsewhere in the poem. Simoeisios' death makes a particularly strong impression on us also because he is only the third character killed in the *Iliad*; the description helps to establish a pattern of meaning that prevents us from simply becoming habituated to or dulled by the many later reports and descriptions of killing and dying:

> Then Ajax son of Telamon killed the son of Anthemion,
> unmarried, blooming Simoeisios, whom once his mother
> coming down from Ida beside the banks of the Simoeis   (475)
> gave birth to, when she followed along with her parents to see
>   the flocks.
> Therefore they called him Simoeisios. Nor did he give a return
> to his dear parents for rearing him, but his life was brief,
> conquered beneath the spear of great-hearted Ajax.
> For as he was moving in the front ranks, Ajax hit him in the
>   chest beside   (480)
> the right nipple; straight through his shoulder the bronze
>   spear
> went, and he fell to the ground in the dust like a black poplar,
> which has grown in the lowland of a great marsh,
> smooth, but its branches grow at the very top;

and which a man who makes chariots cuts down with the
  shining   (485)
iron, so he can bend it into a wheel for a beautiful chariot;
and it lies hardening beside the banks of a river.
Such then was Anthemion's son, Simoeisios, whom Ajax
sprung from Zeus killed.

The passage is framed by statements in lines 473 and 488–89 that Ajax killed Simoeisios. It is notable that Ajax is described as son of Telamon in 473 and merely as "sprung from Zeus," a standard epithet of kings in the *Iliad*, in 489, while Simoeisios in each case is called the son of Anthemion. In the case of Ajax the patronymic merely tells us which Ajax is in action; there is no reason to repeat it. In Simoeisios' case the repeated patronymic calls attention to itself. It suggests the word *anthos*, "flower," thus associating the youth with natural growth.

This botanical association is reinforced by the comparison of Simoeisios' fall beneath Ajax's bronze spear to that of a tree cut down by the "shining iron" of a chariotmaker. Just as the chariotmaker puts an end to a living poplar, which then lies hardening, so Ajax ends the life of the youth, whose body, as corpses do, will grow rigid in death. That the chariotmaker cuts down the tree for a productive purpose, to make an instrument of war, a chariot, is ironically appropriate to Simoeisios' own effort to be a hero in war: he is killed "moving in the front ranks."

Simoeisios, as befits the son of Anthemion, is called "blooming," an etymologically botanical word used elsewhere in the *Iliad* of young men, especially husbands. But he is also "unmarried." We get an idea of a youth both blooming and potentially a husband, of warmth and energy that might have been directed toward a peaceful, fruitful life but were instead turned to war, where death put an end to warmth, flowering, and potential. This sense of unfulfillment is strengthened by the statement that Simoeisios did not repay his dear parents for rearing him.

The vignette about Simoeisios' birth is as moving as the details of his death. Like many other vignettes and similes in the *Iliad*, it moves from the realm of battle and death to a contrasting world of peacetime and everyday life. His mother had been visiting flocks with her parents on Mount Ida, an activity no longer possible during the war, and gave birth to him by the banks of the Simoeis river: one feels the rhythm

of a normal, peaceful pastoral life. There is a particular significance, too, to the river as birthplace. As a source of fertility for the Trojan plain and a landmark associated with the
city, the Simoeis, like the Skamandros, serves as a landscape
symbol for Troy itself. Simoeisios' death is felt, indirectly and
on a small scale, as the death of Troy.

ODYSSEUS KILLS LEODES

Like the Iliad, *the* Odyssey *contains examples of the most
common form of combat death depicted by Homer, that
caused by a single, sudden, decisive blow. In this excerpt from
the scene in which Odysseus slays the suitors, Homer skillfully
builds suspense before supplying the sudden and horrific
description of the deathblow.*

So did Odysseus' party chase the Suitors pell-mell through the
hall and hack them down. Skulls cracked, the hideous groans
of dying men were heard, and the whole floor ran with blood.

Leodes rushed forward, clasped Odysseus' knees and burst
into an anguished appeal: 'I throw myself on your mercy,
Odysseus. Have some regard and pity for me. I swear to you
that never, by word or deed, have I done wrong to a woman in
the house. In fact I did my best to hold them all back from
such evil courses. But they wouldn't listen when I told them to
keep their hands from mischief, and their own iniquities have
brought them to this awful pass. But I was only their priest; I
did nothing. And now I am to share their fate! That is all the
thanks one gets for the goodness one has shown.'

Odysseus looked at him with disgust. 'You say you were
their priest,' he answered. 'How often, then, you must have
prayed in this hall that the happy day of my return might be
put off, and that my dear wife might be yours and bear your
children. For that, nothing shall save you from the bitterness
of death.' And he laid his great hand on a sword dropped on
the ground by Agelaus as he died, and with it struck Leodes
full in the neck, so that his head met the dust before he ceased
to speak.

The poplar's "hardening by the banks of a river" (487),
though in itself not an especially significant detail, echoes
"beside the banks of the Simoeis" (475), thus associating the
fall of the tree more closely with the death of the youth. It almost makes us see the gradual stiffening of his body. Similarly, one can associate the description of the poplar,

"smooth, but its branches grow at the very top," with the appearance of Simoeisios. We visualize the smooth body of an adolescent, entirely without hair except that on his head. This vividness makes the whole scene more poignant; so also does the moving detail that Ajax's spear struck beside the right nipple. The bronze spear, passing straight through the shoulder, coldly destroys what is tender, warm, rooted in life like the poplar. Yet the youth is destroyed by the highest Homeric excellence, heroic *arete* [roughly translated as "personal excellence"], both his own ("moving in the front ranks") and that of Ajax, whose status and glory are based on just such killing of lesser warriors. And the chariot for the sake of which the poplar is cut down is "beautiful."

FOR MORTALS, DEATH IS EVERYTHING

As I have said, the Simoeisios passage is but one of many such vignettes and similes about young men whose deaths Homer narrates. None of the others is so carefully wrought, but each to some extent makes us aware of what the war with its splendid killing costs in human terms. It is significant that almost all of the young victims are Trojans, for the greatest cost of the war is to Troy itself, whose eventual destruction is most clearly prefigured by the death of Hektor. Indeed, Hektor's visit with Andromache and Astyanax in Troy in Book 6 is set in the action of the poem as an expanded vignette of how a man had gone to war leaving his wife and child whom he was never to see again. Homer achieves a similar effect by the description of how Achilles pursued Hektor past the twin springs of Skamandros and the washing troughs "where the wives and beautiful daughters / of the Trojans used to wash their shining garments / before, in peacetime." Homer suspends an image of the normal, domestic life of Troy "before the sons of the Achaians came" in the midst of the climactic episode of the war and of the poem. The effect of this juxtaposition is to remind us of the cost of Achilles' supreme heroic act. Hektor dies fighting not only for glory but also for the life of tender domesticity, characteristically Trojan in the *Iliad*, of which he and Andromache are the poem's prime exemplars.

The description of the death of Simoeisios, like all of Homer's battle narrative, is conventional in style, form, and content; Homer's achievement is the meaning that emerges from this and other such descriptions.... Poems about heroes killing and dying for their own imperishable glory and the sake of their communities seem to be very old in the Indo-European poetic tradition. The formulaic style of the *Iliad*'s battle scenes, as of the rest of the poem, is derived from this tradition. It has been shown, too, that not only descriptions of individuals killing and dying but also the various sequences of Greek and Trojan deaths, and of kinds of wounds, are patterned. In other words, the battle scenes are thematically as well as linguistically formulaic, and they share several other important formal features that would have made them readily intelligible and meaningful to an audience schooled in the conventions of the oral poetic tradition.

For our understanding of the nature and significance of war in the *Iliad*, perhaps the most important shared feature of the numerous scenes of killing and dying is that the combats are generally decided quickly, by one fatal blow. Rarely does a warrior need as many as two moves to finish off an opponent. Correspondingly, those who are hit, with a couple of exceptions, are killed immediately; Homer describes very few nonfatal wounds other than those dealt to the Greek kings in Book 11, when he is motivating the entry of Patroklos and the Myrmidons into the battle. This emphasis on killing rather than wounding shows that Homer is interested not so much in the technique of battle or the detailed, anatomical description of wounds—vivid as this is—as in questions of death itself. Descriptions of warfare are essentially descriptions of death.

On the other hand, the fighting among the gods, and between Diomedes and the gods in Book 5, always results in wounding and never, of course, in a god's death. In contrast to human conflict, which is literally a matter of life and death, divine warfare is a game without serious consequences, a game that . . . can always be replayed. For mortals, death is the end, death is everything.

CHAPTER 2

The *Iliad*: Its Text, Themes, and Characters

READINGS ON
HOMER

The Story of the *Iliad*

Edith Hamilton

One of the great classical scholars of the twentieth century, Edith Hamilton (1867–1963) is fondly remembered for her insightful, beautifully written books on the Greek and Roman world, especially *The Greek Way, The Roman Way*, and *Mythology*. In the following excerpt from *Mythology*, she describes the major events of Homer's *Iliad*, which begins in the tenth year of the Trojan War, a conflict begun after the Trojan prince Paris stole the heart of Spartan king Menelaus's wife, Helen, and boldly brought her to Troy.

The thousand ships carried a great host of fighting men and the Greek Army was very strong, but the Trojan City was strong, too. Priam, the King, and his Queen, Hecuba, had many brave sons to lead the attack and to defend the walls, one above all, Hector, than whom no man anywhere was nobler or more brave, and only one a greater warrior, the champion of the Greeks, Achilles. . . .

For nine years victory wavered, now to this side, now to that. Neither was ever able to gain any decided advantage. Then a quarrel flared up between two Greeks, Achilles and Agamemnon, and for a time it turned the tide in favor of the Trojans. Again a woman was the reason, Chryseis, daughter of Apollo's priest, whom the Greeks had carried off and given to Agamemnon. Her father came to beg for her release, but Agamemnon would not let her go. Then the priest prayed to the mighty god he served and Phoebus Apollo heard him. From his sun-chariot he shot fiery arrows down upon the Greek Army, and men sickened and died so that the funeral pyres were burning continually.

At last Achilles called an assembly of the chieftains. He told them that they could not hold out against both the pestilence and the Trojans, and that they must either find a way to appease Apollo or else sail home. Then the prophet Calchas stood up and said he knew why the god was angry, but that he was afraid to speak unless Achilles would guarantee his safety. "I do so," Achilles answered, "even if you accuse Agamemnon himself." Every man there understood what that meant; they knew how Apollo's priest had been treated. When Calchas declared that Chryseis must be given back to her father, he had all the chiefs behind him and Agamemnon, greatly angered, was obliged to agree. "But if I lose her who was my prize of honor," he told Achilles, "I will have another in her stead."

Therefore when Chryseis had been returned to her father, Agamemnon sent two of his squires to Achilles' tent to take his prize of honor away from him, the maiden Briseis. Most unwillingly they went and stood before the hero in heavy silence. But he knowing their errand told them it was not they who were wronging him. Let them take the girl without fear for themselves, but hear him first while he swore before gods and men that Agamemnon would pay dearly for the deed.

That night Achilles' mother, silver-footed Thetis the sea nymph, came to him. She was as angry as he. She told him to have nothing more to do with the Greeks, and with that she went up to heaven and asked Zeus to give success to the Trojans. Zeus was very reluctant. The war by now had reached Olympus—the gods were ranged against each other. Aphrodite, of course, was on the side of Paris. Equally, of course, Hera and Athena were against him. Ares, God of War, always took sides with Aphrodite; while Poseidon, Lord of the Sea, favored the Greeks, a sea people, always great sailors. Apollo cared for Hector and for his sake helped the Trojans, and Artemis, as his sister, did so too. Zeus liked the Trojans best, on the whole, but he wanted to be neutral because Hera was so disagreeable whenever he opposed her openly. However, he could not resist Thetis. He had a hard time with Hera, who guessed, as she usually did, what he was about. He was driven finally into telling her that he would lay hands upon her if she did not stop talking. Hera kept silence then, but her thoughts were busy as to how she might help the Greeks and circumvent Zeus.

THE EARTH STREAMED WITH BLOOD

The plan Zeus made was simple. He knew that the Greeks without Achilles were inferior to the Trojans, and he sent a

lying dream to Agamemnon promising him victory if he attacked. While Achilles stayed in his tent a fierce battle followed, the hardest yet fought. Up on the wall of Troy the old
King Priam and the other old men, wise in the ways of war,
sat watching the contest . . . until to their astonishment the
battle ceased. The armies drew back on either side and in
the space between, Paris and Menelaus faced each other. It
was evident that the sensible decision had been reached to
let the two most concerned fight it out alone.

Paris struck first, but Menelaus caught the swift spear on
his shield, then hurled his own. It rent Paris' tunic, but did
not wound him. Menelaus drew his sword, his only weapon
now, but as he did so it fell from his hand broken. Un-
daunted though unarmed he leaped upon Paris and seizing
him by his helmet's crest swung him off his feet. He would
have dragged him to the Greeks victoriously if it had not
been for Aphrodite. She tore away the strap that kept the helmet on so that it came away in Menelaus' hand. Paris himself, who had not fought at all except to throw his spear, she
caught up in a cloud and took back to Troy. . . .

The Greeks in rage . . . turned upon the Trojans and the
battle was on again. Terror and Destruction and Strife,
whose fury never slackens, all friends of the murderous
War-god, were there to urge men on to slaughter each other.
Then the voice of groaning was heard and the voice of triumph from slayer and from slain and the earth streamed
with blood.

On the Greek side, with Achilles gone, the two greatest
champions were Ajax and Diomedes. They fought gloriously
that day and many a Trojan lay on his face in the dust before
them. The best and bravest next to Hector, the Prince Aeneas, came near to death at Diomedes' hands. He was of
more than royal blood; his mother was Aphrodite herself,
and when Diomedes wounded him she hastened down to
the battlefield to save him. She lifted him in her soft arms,
but Diomedes, knowing she was a coward goddess, not one
of those who like Athena are masters where warriors fight,
leaped toward her and wounded her hand. Crying out she let
Aeneas fall, and weeping for pain made her way to Olympus,
where Zeus smiling to see the laughter-loving goddess in
tears bade her stay away from battle and remember hers
were the works of love and not of war. But although his
mother failed him Aeneas was not killed. Apollo enveloped

THE FIGHT BETWEEN MENELAUS AND PARIS

In Homer's own words, Paris manages, with the goddess
Aphrodite's help, to escape Menelaus's clutches.

[Menelaus] balanced his long-shadowed spear and hurled it.
The heavy weapon struck the round shield of Priam's son. It
pierced the glittering shield, forced its way through the ornate
cuirass [breastplate], and pressing straight on tore the tunic
on Paris' flank. But Paris swerved, and so avoided death.
Menelaus then drew his silver-mounted sword, swung it back,
and brought it down on the ridge of his enemy's helmet. But
the sword broke on the helmet into half a dozen pieces and
dropped from his hand. Menelaus gave a groan and looked up
at the broad sky. 'Father Zeus,' he cried, 'is there a god more
spiteful than yourself? I thought I had paid out Paris for his
infamy, and now my sword breaks in my hand, when I have
already cast a spear for nothing and never touched the man!'

  With that he hurled himself at Paris, seized him by the
horsehair crest, and swinging him round, began to drag him
into the Achaean lines. Paris was choked by the pressure on
his tender throat of the embroidered helmet-strap, which he
had fitted tightly round his chin; and Menelaus would have
hauled him in and covered himself with glory, but for the
quickness of Aphrodite Daughter of Zeus, who saw what was
happening and broke the strap for Paris, though it was made
of leather from a slaughtered ox. So the helmet came away
empty in the great hand of the noble Menelaus. He tossed it,
with a swing, into the Achaean lines, where it was picked up
by his own retainers, and flung himself at his enemy again in
the hope of despatching him with his bronze-pointed spear.
But Aphrodite used her powers once more. Hiding Paris in a
dense mist, she whisked him off—it was an easy feat for the
goddess—and put him down in his own perfumed fragrant
bedroom.

him in a cloud and carried him to sacred Pergamos, the holy
place of Troy, where Artemis healed him of his wound.

  But Diomedes raged on, working havoc in the Trojan
ranks until he came face to face with Hector. There to his
dismay he saw Ares too. The bloodstained murderous god of
war was fighting for Hector. At the sight Diomedes shud-
dered and cried to the Greeks to fall back, slowly, however,
and with their faces toward the Trojans. Then Hera was
angry. She urged her horses to Olympus and asked Zeus if
she might drive that bane of men, Ares, from the battlefield.

Zeus who loved him no more than Hera did even though he was their son, willingly gave her leave. She hastened down to stand beside Diomedes and urged him to smite the terrible god and have no fear. At that, joy filled the hero's heart. He rushed at Ares and hurled his spear at him. Athena drove it home, and it entered Ares' body. The War-god bellowed as loud as ten thousand cry in battle, and at the awful sound trembling seized the whole host, Greeks and Trojans alike.

Ares, really a bully at heart and unable to bear what he brought upon unnumbered multitudes of men, fled up to Zeus in Olympus and complained bitterly of Athena's violence. But Zeus looked at him sternly and told him he was as intolerable as his mother, and bade him cease his whining. With Ares gone, however, the Trojans were forced to fall back. . . .

HECTOR'S TERRIBLE SPEAR

As Hector went back to the battle he turned aside to see once more, perhaps for the last time, the wife he tenderly loved, Andromache, and his son Astyanax. He met her on the wall where she had gone in terror to watch the fighting when she heard the Trojans were in retreat. With her was a handmaid carrying the little boy. Hector smiled and looked at them silently, but Andromache took his hand in hers and wept. "My dear lord," she said, "you who are father and mother and brother unto me as well as husband, stay here with us. Do not make me a widow and your child an orphan." He refused her gently. He could not be a coward, he said. It was for him to fight always in the forefront of the battle. Yet she could know that he never forgot what her anguish would be when he died. That was the thought that troubled him above all else, more than his many other cares. He turned to leave her, but first he held out his arms to his son. Terrified the little boy shrank back, afraid of the helmet and its fierce nodding crest. Hector laughed and took the shining helmet from his head. Then holding the child in his arms he caressed him and prayed, "O Zeus, in after years may men say of this my son when he returns from battle, 'Far greater is he than his father was.'"

So he laid the boy in his wife's arms and she took him, smiling, yet with tears. And Hector pitied her and touched her tenderly with his hand and spoke to her: "Dear one, be not so sorrowful. That which is fated must come to pass, but against my fate no man can kill me." Then taking up his helmet he left her and she went to her house, often looking back at him and weeping bitterly.

Once again on the battlefield he was eager for the fight, and better fortune for a time lay before him. Zeus had by now remembered his promise to Thetis to avenge Achilles' wrong. He ordered all the other immortals to stay in Olympus; he himself went down to earth to help the Trojans. Then it went hard with the Greeks. Their great champion was far away. Achilles sat alone in his tent, brooding over his wrongs. The great Trojan champion had never before shown himself so brilliant and so brave. Hector seemed irresistible. Tamer of horses, the Trojans always called him, and he drove his car [chariot] through the Greek ranks as if the same spirit animated steeds and driver. His glancing helm was everywhere and one gallant warrior after another fell beneath his terrible bronze spear. When evening ended the battle, the Trojans had driven the Greeks back almost to their ships.

There was rejoicing in Troy that night, but grief and despair in the Greek camp. Agamemnon himself was all for giving up and sailing back to Greece. Nestor, however, who was the oldest among the chieftains and therefore the wisest, wiser even than the shrewd Odysseus, spoke out boldly and told Agamemnon that if he had not angered Achilles they would not have been defeated. "Try to find some way of appeasing him," he said, "instead of going home disgraced." All applauded the advice and Agamemnon confessed that he had acted like a fool. He would send Briseis back, he promised them, and with her many other splendid gifts, and he begged Odysseus to take his offer to Achilles.

BRAVE PATROCLUS'S DOOM SEALED

Odysseus and the two chieftains chosen to accompany him found the hero with his friend Patroclus, who of all men on earth was dearest to him. Achilles welcomed them courteously and set food and drink before them, but when they told him why they had come and all the rich gifts that would be his if he would yield, and begged him to have pity on his hard-pressed countrymen, they received an absolute refusal. Not all the treasures of Egypt could buy him, he told them. He was sailing home and they would be wise to do the same.

But all rejected that counsel when Odysseus brought back the answer. The next day they went into battle with the desperate courage of brave men cornered. Again they were driven back, until they stood fighting on the beach where their ships were drawn up. . . .

They fled in confusion to the ships, and the wall they had built to defend them went down like a sand wall children heap up on the shore and then scatter in their play. The Trojans were almost near enough to set the ships on fire. The Greeks, hopeless, thought only of dying bravely.

Patroclus, Achilles' beloved friend, saw the rout with horror. Not even for Achilles' sake could he stay longer away from the battle. "You can keep your wrath while your countrymen go down in ruin," he cried to Achilles. "I cannot. Give me your armor. If they think I am you, the Trojans may pause and the worn-out Greeks have a breathing space. You and I are fresh. We might yet drive back the enemy. But if you will sit nursing your anger, at least let me have the armor." As he spoke one of the Greek ships burst into flame. "That way they can cut off the Army's retreat," Achilles said. "Go. Take my armor, my men too, and defend the ships. I cannot go. I am a man dishonored. For my own ships, if the battle comes near them, I will fight. I will not fight for men who have disgraced me."

So Patroclus put on the splendid armor all the Trojans knew and feared, and led the Myrmidons, Achilles' men, to the battle. At the first onset of this new band of warriors the Trojans wavered; they thought Achilles led them on. And indeed for a time Patroclus fought as gloriously as that great hero himself could have done. But at last he met Hector face to face and his doom was sealed as surely as a boar is doomed when he faces a lion. Hector's spear gave him a mortal wound and his soul fled from his body down to the house of Hades. Then Hector stripped his armor from him and casting his own aside, put it on. It seemed as though he had taken on, too, Achilles' strength, and no man of the Greeks could stand before him.

ACHILLES BACK IN THE FIGHT

Evening came that puts an end to battle. Achilles sat by his tent waiting for Patroclus to return. But instead he saw old Nestor's son running toward him, fleet-footed Antilochus. He was weeping hot tears as he ran. "Bitter tidings," he cried out. "Patroclus is fallen and Hector has his armor." Grief took hold of Achilles, so black that those around him feared for his life. Down in the sea caves his mother knew his sorrow and came up to try to comfort him. . . .

"Only wait until morning," she said, "and you will not go unarmed to battle. I will bring you arms fashioned by the divine armorer, the god Hephaestus himself."

Marvelous arms they were when Thetis brought them, worthy of their maker, such as no man on earth had ever borne. The Myrmidons gazed at them with awe and a flame of fierce joy blazed in Achilles' eyes as he put them on. Then at last he left the tent in which he had sat so long, and went down to where the Greeks were gathered, a wretched company, Diomedes grievously wounded, Odysseus, Agamemnon, and many another. He felt shame before them and he told them he saw his own exceeding folly in allowing the loss of a mere girl to make him forget everything else. But that was over; he was ready to lead them as before. Let them prepare at once for the battle. . . .

The Trojans under Hector fought as brave men fight before the walls of their home. Even the great river of Troy, which the gods call Xanthus and men Scamander, took part and strove to drown Achilles as he crossed its waters. In vain, for nothing could check him as he rushed on slaughtering all in his path and seeking everywhere for Hector. The gods by now were fighting, too, as hotly as the men, and Zeus sitting apart in Olympus laughed pleasantly to himself when he saw god matched against god: Athena felling Ares to the ground; Hera seizing the bow of Artemis from her shoulders and boxing her ears with it this way and that; Poseidon provoking Apollo with taunting words to strike him first. The Sun-god refused the challenge. He knew it was of no use now to fight for Hector.

THE DEATH OF HECTOR

By this time the gates, the great Scaean gates of Troy, had been flung wide, for the Trojans at last were in full flight and were crowding into the town. Only Hector stood immovable before the wall. From the gates old Priam, his father, and his mother Hecuba cried to him to come within and save himself, but he did not heed. He was thinking, "I led the Trojans. Their defeat is my fault. . . . Better to join battle with him now even if I die."

On came Achilles, glorious as the sun when he rises. Beside him was Athena, but Hector was alone. Apollo had left him to his fate. As the pair drew near he turned and fled. Three times around the wall of Troy pursued and pursuer ran with flying feet. It was Athena who made Hector halt. She appeared beside him in the shape of his brother, Deiphobus, and with this ally as he thought, Hector faced Achilles. He cried out to him, "If I kill you I will give back your body to your friends and do you do the same to me." But Achilles answered, "Madman. There are no covenants between sheep and wolves, nor between you and me." So saying he hurled his spear. It missed its aim, but Athena brought it back. Then Hector struck with a true aim; the spear hit the center of Achilles' shield. But to what good? That armor was magical and could not be pierced. He turned quickly to Deiphobus to get his spear, but he was not there. Then Hector knew the truth. Athena had tricked him and there was no way of escape. "The gods have summoned me to death," he thought. "At least I will not die without a struggle, but in some great deed of arms which men yet to be born will tell each other." He drew his sword, his only weapon now, and rushed upon his enemy. But Achilles had a spear, the one Athena had recovered for him. Before Hector could approach, he who knew well that armor taken by Hector from the dead Patroclus aimed at an opening in it near the throat, and drove the spearpoint in. Hector fell, dying at last. With his last breath he prayed, "Give back my body to my father and my mother." "No prayers from you to me, you dog," Achilles answered. "I would that I could make myself devour raw your flesh for the evil you have brought upon me." Then Hector's soul flew forth from his body and was gone to Hades, bewailing his fate, leaving vigor and youth behind.

Achilles stripped the bloody armor from the corpse while the Greeks ran up to wonder how tall he was as he lay there and how noble to look upon. But Achilles' mind was on other matters. He pierced the feet of the dead man and fastened them with thongs to the back of his chariot, letting the head trail. Then he lashed his horses and round and round the walls of Troy he dragged all that was left of glorious Hector. . . .

Up in Olympus there was dissension. This abuse of the dead displeased all the immortals except Hera and Athena and Poseidon. Especially it displeased Zeus. He sent Iris [his messenger goddess] to Priam, to order him to go without fear to Achilles to redeem Hector's body, bearing a rich ransom. She was to tell him that violent as Achilles was, he was not really evil, but one who would treat properly a suppliant.

Then the aged King heaped a car with splendid treasures, the best in Troy, and went over the plain to the Greek camp. Hermes met him, looking like a Greek youth and offering himself as a guide to Achilles' tent. So accompanied the old man passed the guards and came into the presence of the man who had killed and maltreated his son. He clasped his knees and kissed his hands and as he did so Achilles felt awe and so did all the others there, looking strangely upon one another. "Remember, Achilles," Priam said, "your own father, of like years with me and like me wretched for want of a son. Yet I am by far more to be pitied who have braved what no man on earth ever did before, to stretch out my hand to the slayer of my son."

Grief stirred within Achilles' heart as he listened. Gently he raised the old man. "Sit by me here," he said, "and let our sorrow lie quiet in our hearts. Evil is all men's lot, but yet we must keep courage." Then he bade his servant wash and anoint Hector's body and cover it with a soft robe, so that Priam should not see it, frightfully mangled as it was.... Then Priam brought Hector home, mourned in Troy as never another....

Nine days they lamented him; then they laid him on a lofty pyre and set fire to it. When all was burned they quenched the flame with wine and gathered the bones into a golden urn, shrouding them in soft purple. They set the urn in a hollow grave and piled great stones over it.

This was the funeral of Hector, tamer of horses.

And with it the *Iliad* ends.

The *Iliad* and the Heroic Ideal

Michael Grant

Michael Grant, formerly of Queen's University,
Belfast, and one of the twentieth century's most
prolific and respected classical historians, here
makes the case that one of the lasting legacies of
Homer's *Iliad* to Western civilization is the concept
of a larger-than-life hero. Homeric heroes like
Achilles, says Grant, lived and died by a strict code
of honor and idealized such qualities as courage,
strength, and beauty. In this view, the ideal hero
is a person who struggles relentlessly against the
workings of fate, and in the process manages,
even if briefly, to rise above the fragile, vulgar,
and ignoble aspects of human nature.

One of the *Iliad*'s outstanding contributions to human civilization, for good and for evil, is its concept of the hero. The
Greeks of the eighth century B.C., and for ever afterwards, saw
something splendid and superhuman about what they supposed to be their lost past. This seemed to them filled with su-
perb figures living for renown, and pursuing it with competitive vigour. The hero must use his superior qualities at all
times to excel and win applause, for that is the reward and
demonstration of his manhood. He makes honour his paramount code, and glory the driving force and aim of his existence. Birth, wealth and prowess confirm a hero's title; his
ideals are courage, endurance, strength and beauty. Enthusi-
astically confident in what he achieves and possesses, he re-
lies upon his own ability to make the fullest use of his powers.

Yet, although he is no god, there is something about him
which brings him not too far from heaven: Hesiod [the
seventh-century Greek who wrote about the gods in his
Theogony] thought of the heroes as half-way between gods

and men. Their mighty achievements inspired poets to suggest that human nature, far though it is from divinity, can yet come within reach of it—a conclusion which the greater claims of the supernatural had made impossible for Egypt or Babylonia. For the Greeks, too, there were many reserves and qualifications; yet man could still aspire. In the words of Pindar the Boeotian:

> We can in greatness of mind
> Or of body be like the Immortals,
> Though we know not to what goal
> By day or in the nights
> Fate has written that we shall run.

Glory—favourable public opinion—was the quality by which the individual could become like the gods. It was a glory of military and athletic prowess, hereditary arrogance and aristocratic class privilege. The only demagogue in the *Iliad*, Thersites, receives contemptuous punishment. Heroic aspiration is the keynote; denial of due honour was a catastrophe for Achilles. The hero's whole career was an unremitting struggle, undertaken with all his manly endurance (*tlemosyne*), for the first prize among his peers. In a period of rapid transition Homer, like Dante and Shakespeare after him, is upholding a traditional nostalgic system of values.

No remote serenity was attributed to these legendary figures. They were violently emotional, and of erratic temperamental stability. When Patroclus is killed, there is no question of the greatest of the heroes, Achilles, keeping a stiff upper lip. "He picked up the dark dust in both his hands and poured it on his head. He soiled his comely face with it, and filthy ashes settled on his scented tunic. He cast himself down on the earth and lay there like a fallen giant, fouling his hair and tearing it out with his own hands. The maidservants whom he and Patroclus had captured caught the alarm and all ran screaming out of doors. They beat their breasts with their hands and sank to the ground beside their royal master. On the other side, Antilochus shedding tears of misery held the hands of Achilles as he sobbed out his noble heart, for fear that he might take a knife and cut his throat."

Yet in weakness and strength alike the Hero has transformed our ways of thinking. The heroic outlook shook off primitive superstitions and taboos by showing that man can do amazing things by his own effort and by his own nature, indeed that he can almost rise *above* his own nature into strengths scarcely known or understood. As early as the Homeric poems themselves the great stories are held up as educational examples. This continued throughout antiquity, and then again in the schools of the Renaissance upon which the *élite* institutions of today, not least in Britain and America, are still based. When we read the *Iliad*, we feel larger than life, freed from the compulsion of present realities. The epic heroes carry us with them in their struggles and their sufferings; they are not as we are, yet we follow after them. And so when they suffer or exult, so do we. . . .

A GLORIOUS BLOODBATH

Yet much of the militancy of the western tradition, as well as its humanity, can also be traced back to the personages of the *Iliad;* . . . for the Homeric hero loved battle, and fighting was his life. The society to which he is said to belong devotes peculiar, maximum attention to war, like the heroic ages in Russia, India, among the south Slavs, and also (we are learning) in Africa. A hero's activity is narrower than a god's because it is concentrated on the most testing kind of action, war—hateful perhaps and with miserable moments, but an unequalled field for achievement and glory. Large stretches of the *Iliad* have been described as a bath of blood, gloriously described. The fighting can occasionally be broken off for a conference (*Iliad* II, III). But, although there are subordinate traces of a more peaceful ethic embodying ideas of justice, the heroic pursuit of glory leaves no room for chivalry or the sporting spirit, because lack of suitably emphasized vengeance would mean an inadequate satisfaction of honour. It was, usually, futile to plead with a hero's sense of injury. "Patroclus picked up a jagged, sparkling stone— his hand just covered it—and standing in no awe of Hector threw it with all his force. He did not make an idle cast, for the sharp stone caught Hector's driver Cebriones, King Priam's bastard son, on the forehead, with the horses' reins in his hands. It shattered both his eyebrows, crushing in the bone; and his eyes fell out and rolled in the dust at his feet. He dropped from the well-built chariot like a diver and yielded up his life. The knight Patroclus jeered at him: 'Ha! Quite an acrobat, I see, judging by that graceful dive! The man who takes so neat a header from a chariot on land could dive for oysters from a ship at sea in any weather and fetch up plenty for a feast. I did not know that the Trojans had such divers.'"

The gloating reaches its culmination when Achilles and Hector meet in the duel that is fatal to Hector.

Clean through the soft part of the neck the spearpoint was driven.
Yet the ash spear heavy with bronze did not sever the windpipe,
so that Hector could still make exchange of words spoken.
But he dropped in the dust, and brilliant Achilles vaunted above him:
"Hector, surely you thought as you killed Patroclus you would be
safe, and since I was far away you thought nothing of me,
o fool, for an avenger was left, far greater than he was,
behind him and away by the hollow ships. And it was I;
and I have broken your strength; on you the dogs and the vultures
shall feed and foully rip you; the Achaeans will bury Patroclus."

And Achilles, each day, dragged the corpse in the dust behind his chariot, three times round the tomb of Patroclus. Already at the funeral of Patroclus, Achilles in his grief had gone beyond the Homeric norm—by human sacrifice. He had "done an evil thing: he put a dozen brave men, the sons of noble Trojans, to the sword, and set the pyre alight so that pitiless flames might feed on them." Genocide, too, already thousands of years old, had been the stated aim of the Trojan War as Homer described it. "No, we are not going to leave a single one of them alive, down to the babies in their mothers' wombs—not even they must live. The whole people must be wiped out of existence, and none be left to think of them and shed a tear."

HEROISM LEADS TO DEATH

Such barbarities apart, an atmosphere of tragedy surrounds the Hero. There is pathos in his struggle against his fellows and against fate; he fulfills himself in death, the last and most searching ordeal, the true test of worth. The death of the old in battle, thought Homer and after him the Spartan poet Tyrtaeus, was even more to be deplored than the death of the young, for the old man's corpse looks less noble. But the death of a hero, too, was seen as utterly hateful. . . . Heroism leads to misery and death, honour to slaughter: the poet knows much about human suffering. Such a myth . . . reflects human nature's tragic ambivalence, of which there is no termination but death.

The epic bards of all nations inherited a tradition of sorrow and defeat. And above all the deaths of Hector and Patroclus, for all the bragging over them, are too pitiful for savage exultation to prevail. There is pity for the shortness of heroes' lives and the waste caused by their anger and pride, and pity is heightened by the contrast between their passionate delight in living and our knowledge (which they sometimes share) of what lies in store for them. Yet this is ... a conviction based less on pessimism than on the belief that life is important because there is little beyond the grave. The pathos and war weariness of the *Iliad* are subordinate to the main clash of arms; nevertheless, at times, the sadness is clearly heard. It is a tragic conception, already sounded in the first five verses, that a quarrel should bring so much death and disaster.

No Tidy Answer to the Question of Heroism

In this excerpt from his book Homer: The Iliad, *scholar M.S. Silk suggests that Homer's vision of heroism is complex, combining optimism about striving for glorious achievement with pessimism about the miserable lot destiny has preordained for humanity.*

Heroic ideology insists on a special kind of optimism: the quest for glory presupposes a bleak acceptance that this life is all the life we have, but also the hope of a secondary immortality, for the favoured few, through achievement. Yet Achilles, the supreme achiever, sums up his experience of life, not in terms of glory and hope, but through the image of the urns of Zeus [in which humans are described as "wretched things," into whose lives the gods have "woven sorrow"]. That image promises blessings as well as afflictions, but afflictions predominate and, in particular, nothing is said of any permanent consolation.

We might suppose that, in the context of such a pessimistic summing-up, immortal achievement and the consolation it yields should become yet more precious, but Achilles neither says this nor denies it. A tidy answer misrepresents the poem. Heroic endeavour *and* Achilles' eccentric version of it are both offered as realities. Homer's presentation of war subsumes the heroic attitude, along with others. His presentation of Achilles includes both a contribution to heroism and a challenge to it.

On the Trojan side, there is impending catastrophe in Hector's meeting with his baby boy Astyanax.

> But may I be dead and the piled earth hide me
>   under before I
> hear you crying and know by this that they drag
>   you captive. . . .

The chain of events that had begun with the old father of Chryseis hounded from the Greek camp ends with Hector's old father being sent home, by the most ferocious of heroes, with mercy. That meeting of Achilles, at the end of the poem, with the bereaved father of his enemy is in profound contrast to slaughter and human sacrifice; it is like the Reversal or Recoil which was later to be the hallmark of many an Athenian tragedy. The ostensibly simple description of this scene is all the more pathetic because the dominant note of the whole poem still remains, not pathos, but the roar and exultation of battle. Out of the degradation and misery comes compassion.

Such compassionate chords make up the profound humanity of the *Iliad.* Though scarcely pointing any moral, the poem (with a magical blend of simplicity and grandeur) justifies the ways of men and women at their finest and best. These myths did much to launch the Greeks upon their abiding concern with human dignity. The view is impersonal and disengaged, yet interpretation of thoughts and motives is both lively and understanding, tolerant but never indifferent, passionate but balanced. Far above the level of saga, the *Iliad* combines the unfaltering vision of Dante with Shakespeare's boundless sympathy. Men are unscrupulous, hot-tempered, irresolute and domineering, but they are also noble, self-sacrificing, impelled by deep emotions, and devoted to an exacting code.

Already in the Homeric poems themselves its stories are held up as educational models and sagas for the attention of posterity; and part of the significance of the Trojan myth lies in the variety of responses that it has evoked from creative imaginations throughout the ages. Achilles and the rest have been needed, at many epochs, to invigorate men's perceptions of their own surroundings. To this day they provide, as [Homeric scholar Sir John] Myres expressed it, "an enlargement, disentanglement and articulation of our own experience."

Achilles: An Exceptional Hero Gains Self-Awareness

M.S. Silk

Achilles is the central character of Homer's *Iliad*.
While he sulks day after day in his tent, refusing to
lead the Greeks in battle, the life-and-death struggles
of other heroes, often influenced and manipulated
by the gods, swirl relentlessly around him, until
finally, shocked into action by the death of his friend
Patroclus, he reenters the fray. In this essay, M.S.
Silk, Reader in Classics, King's College, London,
and author of the informative *Homer: The Iliad*,
examines the many facets of this exceptional hero's
character, focusing on his ability to change from a
"vengeful killer" to a "heightened form of humanity."
Silk makes the point that the action of the story
forces Achilles to discover and face who he really
is, an example of masterful character development
rarely equaled in literature.

Achilles is special. He weeps with wretched Priam, his
enemy, as they share their different griefs.... Achilles killed
Hector to avenge Patroclus. Patroclus' death was his responsibility, for which only that revenge-killing could make
amends. By that revenge, however, Achilles has ensured, in
full consciousness, that he cannot...reach his homeland
again. This is his personal sorrow, which, out of consideration for Priam, he declines to articulate, however painful such
silence must be for a 'plain-speaking' hero; his anger reflects
that pain and the underlying sorrow in one. All of which
makes Achilles, and his presentation, unique in the *Iliad*.

Achilles is the only character in the poem to be explored
in any depth. He is the only character who can really be
shown to possess such depth. Why this should be is a matter

for speculation, but we may note: that Achilles motivates the action of the poem, and is, therefore, a focus of interest in his own right; that his specific decision to withdraw from the fighting requires him to articulate his already unusual situation, and so reveal himself to himself, as others are never required to; that it is an exceptional and extreme self that he reveals; but that without the special pressures of war (we infer) even this exceptional person would not be brought to this revelation.

A Man 'Utterly Out of Season'

This exceptional hero has a suitably special, even alien, background. His mother is a sea-nymph and he was brought up by a centaur, Chiron. And during the action these alien connections are evoked by his god-made weapons, his talking horse, his fight with a river.

By background, he is alien; by temperament, swift. He becomes an outsider. The key-word for understanding him is the surprising word he applies to himself in the Priam scene: *panaórios*: a word evidently coined for this context, and hinting at an untimely death, but in itself meaning 'utterly out of season', therefore at odds with natural rhythms and norms.

Unlike his great enemy Hector, the outsider Achilles is rootless. He has no family near him and no friends, except for one close friend. We see him leave the war, then rejoin the war, as the individualist hero *par excellence*; and before he rejoins the war, we see him sitting on the sea-shore on his own, spurning the assembly where men meet, as well as the war where they fight; we even see him, with Patroclus as his silent audience, playing the convivial lyre on his own.

And the outsider becomes an extremist in all things. On hearing the news of Patroclus' death, he tears his hair and rolls in ashes, and days later he is still refusing food and sex with his woman, Briseis. And yet he is as intense a lover of Briseis as he was a friend of Patroclus, whom he honoured as he honoured himself. When she is taken from him, he grieves for her; he calls her his wife, his darling; she was only the spoils of war, but he loved her from the heart. When Hector acknowledges his supremacy and supplicates him, his response is to wish he could eat his enemy alive, and his actual treatment of Hector's body scandalises the gods. His refusal to accept Agamemnon's generous settlement violates expectation and precedent, as Phoenix and Ajax make clear.

With his extreme temperament and his propensity for isolation, Achilles finds himself in a unique situation. The greatest of the heroes becomes the most obdurate anti-hero; but the heroic life provides no practice in opting out of wars, and by opting out of this war, Achilles exposes himself to contradictory feelings, which he expresses by contradictory actions. Withdrawn to his tent, he longs for the war, but he also longs for home: his speech to Odysseus in the embassy-scene contains a plaintive fantasia on the theme of a marriage in his native 'Hellas and Phthia'. Athene stays his hand against Agamemnon with the promise of great gifts in the future; when Agamemnon offers them, he scorns them; later, the same gifts seem to be uppermost in his thoughts; finally, when he does decide to rejoin the war, and Agamemnon assures him that the promised gifts will still be his, they seem, after all, hardly to concern him. Before Patroclus' death he entertains the wish that the whole Achaean army should perish along with Troy, and that he and Patroclus alone should survive; after Patroclus' death he laments that he gave no assistance to Patroclus himself *or* to his other comrades. Briseis is his 'wife', his 'darling'; but when he makes his peace with Agamemnon, she is just 'a girl' who should have died the day he first captured her, and saved so many Achaean lives. Even his extreme actions may oscillate, contradictorily, from one extreme to another. . . . After Patroclus' death he kills all his victims and kills and mutilates the suppliant Hector; after Hector's death, humanity returns, and he responds to Priam's entreaties, which no other hero in fact does for a defeated enemy in the *Iliad.*

A Crisis of Choice

Our understanding of this extraordinary character is enhanced by an unusual amount of information about his background. His own speeches provide much of this, but we hear a good deal also from less predictable sources, like Andromache, Phoenix, Nestor, and Odysseus. . . . Above all, we learn from Achilles himself about his fate, his awareness of that fate, and the unique personal crisis that this awareness represents, a crisis of choice and even—in this one instance—a crisis of conscience, to which all his contradictory feelings and actions can be traced: 'my mother . . . tells me I have two destinies. . . . If I stay here, waging war on Troy, my hope of home is lost, but I win immortal glory. If I get back home to my own land, fine glory is lost, but my life will be long . . .'. Possessed of this knowledge, Achilles must choose. His original inclination must have been to choose glory and a short life at Troy. The strength of his grudge against Agamemnon leads him towards the alternative. In his speech to Odysseus in IX he actually talks as if he has now opted for life: 'tomorrow I shall . . . load my ships and put to sea, and at daybreak, if you care to look, you will see them sailing over the Hellespont'. However, his next speech, to Phoenix, leaves it open: 'at daybreak we shall decide whether to go home or stay'. And his next, to Ajax, is different again. He is apparently thinking of staying put after all, but—'I will not bother myself with bloody war until great Hector . . . kills his way to the huts and the ships of the Myrmidons, and sets the ships on fire'. Whether this plan, which he later reaffirms to Patroclus, was always his real intention, we are not invited to consider. What is significant is the sequence of contradictory positions, so eloquent of the great hero's indecision. The plan is, in any case, not to be realised: it is Patroclus who re-enters the war in Achilles' stead, when Hector does fire the first ship, and Achilles himself joins in only later to avenge his friend. That belated re-entry, however, marks his final decision to die at Troy, and is so interpreted both by Achilles' goddess mother and by Achilles himself. . . .

SPECIAL INSIGHTS AND EXPRESSIVE SPEECH

Achilles' special consciousness is not confined to his own fate. When a hero is dying and making his death-speech, he is often credited with a kind of momentary insight such as a god might possess—as if the human spirit, on its way from earth to the divine, if dismal, realms of the underworld, experienced a flash of divine omniscience. So Hector, as he dies, warns Achilles of 'that day when Paris and Phoebus Apollo will kill you, for all your greatness, at the Scaean gate'. Achilles alone enjoys, or suffers, that special insight while he still lives, and in his confrontation with Priam in XXIV this insight at last takes a positive form. In the image of the urns of Zeus, it translates itself into a profound statement about the human condition, which no one else is fitted to articulate; and it is informed by a powerful humanity. . . . For with his consciousness of life, Achilles gains a rare self-awareness, typified by the elaborate manoeuvre with the

body which is designed to ensure that Priam does not un-
wittingly provoke him again.

ACHILLES AND PRIAM LAMENT TOGETHER

*Here is E.V. Rieu's translation of the magnificent scene in
which Achilles and his enemy King Priam console each
other about their personal losses and the cruelties of fate.*

Priam had set Achilles thinking of his own father and brought
him to the verge of tears. Taking the old man's hand, he gently put him from him; and overcome by their memories they
both broke down. Priam, crouching at Achilles' feet, wept bitterly for man-slaying Hector, and Achilles wept for his father,
and then again for Patroclus. The house was filled with the
sounds of their lamentation. But presently, when he had had
enough of tears and recovered his composure, the excellent
Achilles leapt from his chair, and in compassion for the old
man's grey head and grey beard, took him by the arm and
raised him. Then he spoke to him from his heart: 'You are indeed a man of sorrows and have suffered much. How could
you dare to come by yourself to the Achaean ships into the
presence of a man who has killed so many of your gallant
sons? You have a heart of iron. But pray be seated now, here
on this chair, and let us leave our sorrows, bitter though they
are, locked up in our own hearts, for weeping is cold comfort
and does little good. We men are wretched things, and the
gods, who have no cares themselves, have woven sorrow into
the very pattern of our lives. You know that Zeus the Thunderer has two jars standing on the floor of his Palace, in
which he keeps his gifts, the evils in one and the blessings in
the other. People who receive from him a mixture of the two
have varying fortunes, sometimes good and sometimes bad,
though when Zeus serves a man from the jar of evil only, he
makes him an outcast, who is chased by the gadfly of despair
over the face of the earth and goes his way damned by gods
and men alike.

The special hero is special in another way. Despite the
levelling effect of formulaic style, he talks differently from
any other character.... Achilles is also given to using similes, which in general belong to the expressive repertoire of
the narrative, and one of these is particularly noteworthy.
The narrator frequently represents the heroes as maraud-
ing, inhuman lions, and in his combat with Hector, Achilles
sees himself, as opposed to his opponent, in this role. Before

they fight, Hector proposes that they agree to one thing: the winner should return the body of the loser to his own people. Achilles refuses: 'Hector, you are mad to talk to me of agreements: there are no oaths of faith between lions and men . . .'. For Achilles, as for an omniscient narrator, he is the lion and Hector the man. It is significant that when he responds adversely to Priam, in the consciousness of his situation, he springs from the room, again, 'like a lion'—which is the last of all the similes in the poem.

ACHIEVING THE PROPER EMOTIONAL BALANCE

Between the killing and mutilation of Hector and the heightened encounter with Priam, Achilles is seen in two different roles. He organises the funeral for Patroclus and he presides at the funeral games. As the cremation ritual is completed, Achilles wails:

> As a father wails for his son, when he burns his bones, a son newly married, whose death has brought grief to his unhappy parents, so Achilles wailed for his friend, as he burned his bones, dragging his feet round the pyre, groaning.
>
> (XXIII 222ff.)

Achilles weeps for Patroclus as father for son, as if by some symbolic identification with Priam grieving for Hector, as he will identify with him in XXIV. Then, at the games, Achilles assumes the role of umpire. Quarrels break out among the spectators, and he deals with them. . . .

In XXII Achilles is a vengeful killer; in XXIV he is a heightened form of humanity, participating in an extraordinary relationship with his enemy, Priam: the instinctive hero of I has been forced into a momentous self-awareness. The characters in the *Iliad* do not, even cannot, show personal development; and yet Achilles' switch from killer to man—*via* his activities in XXIII—looks remarkably like it. Sensitive critics grope for the right answer. Some talk of Achilles' 'maturation', as if it were a process and a natural movement up the pre-ordained ages of man. . . . The truth (we would argue) is that Achilles does, uniquely, 'develop', but that this 'development' is represented not as a process, let alone a natural one, but as a series of responses to experience, many of them excessive. On his first appearance in the *Iliad*, in I before the quarrel, Achilles is courteous and responsible. When Apollo's plague afflicts the Achaeans, it is Achilles who summons an assembly to consider its cause.

His hot temper is soon apparent, of course, but so it is in his encounter with Priam. It is as if his 'mature' response to Priam is conceived of as the restoration of a proper emotional balance ... without reference to his new consciousness at all. Yet this consciousness is a fact, and a formative one. That Achilles can characterise his present relationship with Priam as 'squatting here at Troy, afflicting you and your children' implies a remarkable distance from himself, which the idiomatic and almost dismissively brusque 'squatting' seems to enforce. What he undergoes and achieves is unique in the poem and, so far as we know, for some centuries to come.

Helen: A Prisoner of Her Own Beauty

Rachel Bespaloff

Wound up in the incessant battles for honor and other male-centered action of the *Iliad*, many critics have neglected the importance of the mortal female characters (plenty of attention is given to the goddesses Hera, Athena, and Aphrodite, who aid their human champions), including Helen, whose beauty, after all, caused the war in the first place. In this essay, Rachel Bespaloff, noted philosopher, essayist, and author of the insightful book *On the Iliad*, addresses the famous Helen of Troy. Bespaloff contends that, though Helen's enchanting beauty constitutes a wonderful gift from the gods, it is also a curse, for Greeks and Trojans alike desire her and fight over her; and no matter who wins the war, in the end she will not have the luxury of choosing her mate, but will have to go with the winner. A pawn of both humans and gods, she must live with the knowledge that her good looks are as much a trap as a boon.

Of all the figures in the poem she is the severest, the most austere. Shrouded in her long white veils, Helen walks across the *Iliad* like a penitent; misfortune and beauty are consummate in her and lend majesty to her step. For this royal recluse freedom does not exist; the very slave who numbers the days of oppression on some calendar of hope is freer than she. What has Helen to hope for? Nothing short of the death of the Immortals would restore her freedom, since it is the gods, not her fellow men, who have dared to put her in bondage. Her fate does not depend on the outcome of the war; Paris or Menelaus may get her, but for her nothing can really change. She is the prisoner of the passions her beauty

Excerpted from Rachel Bespaloff's "Helen," in *Homer: A Collection of Critical Essays*, edited by George Steiner and Robert Fagles. Copyright ©1947 by Princeton University Press. Reprinted by permission of Princeton University Press.

excited, and her passivity is, so to speak, their underside. Aphrodite rules her despotically; the goddess commands and Helen bows, whatever her private repugnance. Pleasure is extorted from her; this merely makes her humiliation the more cruel. Her only resource is to turn against herself a wrath too weak to spite the gods. She seems to live in horror of herself. "Why did I not die before?" is the lament that keeps rising to her lips. Homer is as implacable toward Helen as [Russian novelist Leo] Tolstoy is toward Anna [in his novel *Anna Karenina*]. Both women have run away from home thinking that they could abolish the past and capture the future in some unchanging essence of love. They awake in exile and feel nothing but a dull disgust for the shrivelled ecstasy that has outlived their hope. The promise of freedom has been sloughed off in servitude; love does not obey the rules of love but yields to some more ancient and ruder law. Beauty and death have become neighbors and from their alliance springs a necessity akin to that of force. When Helen and Anna come to and face their deteriorated dream, they can blame only themselves for having been the dupes of harsh Aphrodite. Everything they squandered comes back on them; everything they touch turns to dust or stone. In driving his heroine to suicide, Tolstoy goes beyond Christianity and rejoins Homer and the tragic poets. To them the hero's flaw is indistinguishable from the misery that arises from it. The sufferer bears it; he pays for it, but he cannot redeem it any more than he can live his life over. Clytemnestra, Orestes, and Oedipus [mythical Greek characters who commit murder and suffer the punishment of the gods] are their crimes; they have no existence outside them. Later on, the philosophers, heirs of Odysseus, introduce the Trojan horse of dialectic into the realm of tragedy. Error takes the place of the tragic fault, and the responsibility for it rests with the individual alone. With Homer, punishment and expiation have the opposite effect; far from fixing responsibility, they dissolve it in the vast sea of human suffering and the diffuse guilt of the life-process itself. A flaw in a defective universe is not quite the same thing as a sin; remorse and grace have not yet made their appearance. But it is nonetheless true that this Greek idea of a diffuse guilt represents for Homer and the tragic poets the equivalent of the Christian idea of original sin. Fed on the same reality, charged with the same weight of experience, it contains the same appraisal of existence. It too acknowledges a fall, but a fall that has no date and has been preceded by no state of innocence and will be followed by no redemption; the fall, here, is a continuous one as the life-process itself which heads forever downward into death and the absurd. . . . If the final responsibility for the tragic guilt rests on the mischievous gods, this does not mean that guilt is nonexistent. On the contrary, there is not a page in the *Iliad* that does not emphasize its irreducible character. So fully does Helen assume it that she does not even permit herself the comfort of self-defense. In Helen, purity and guilt mingle confusedly as they do in the vast heart of the warrior herd spread out on the plain at her feet.

HELEN AND HECTOR

Thus Helen, at Ilion [Troy], drags her ill luck along with a kind of somber humility that still makes no truce with the gods. But is it really Aphrodite? Is it not rather the Asiatic Astarte who has trapped her? In a certain way, Helen's destiny prefigures that of Greece which, from the Trojan War to Alexander's conquests, was alternately submitting to and repelling the tremendous attraction of the Orient. What the exile misses in Paris' high dwelling is not the blond Achaean, arrogant Menelaus, son of a wild race of Northern barbarians, but the rude, pure homeland—the familiar city, the child she used to fondle.

How tired she gets of the soft, weak ways of Aphrodite's protégé [Prince Paris]; he is a humiliation and a wound to her. "If the gods have decreed these evils for us, why could not I have had a husband who was capable of a feeling of revolt?" Here in hostile Troy, where boredom makes her despondent, Helen has no one to cling to but Hector, the least oriental of Priam's sons, the most manly, the most Greek. There is a feeling of tenderness between them. Helen's presence is odious to everyone, and Hector is her only defender from the hatred she excites. Nobody can forgive the stranger for being the embodiment of the fatality that pursues the city. Innocent though she is, Helen feels the weight of these rebukes; she even seems to invite them, as though courting a just punishment for a crime she did not commit. She is all the more grateful, therefore, to the one person who shows her compassion without importuning her with lust. When Hector comes to scold Paris, Helen is worried about the dangers that threaten her brother-in-law. He is the only one to whom she speaks gently: "Meanwhile, come in, brother, and take this seat. Care assails your heart more than anyone else's, and that because of me, bitch that I am, and the folly of Alexander. Zeus has given us a hard lot, that later on we may be the subject of a song for men to come." These words weave a complicity between Hector and Helen that is something more than fraternal. With an unequalled insight, Homer hears in their talk an accent of intimacy which is attuned to the truth of human relationships. This affection, on Helen's part at least, shields a deeper feeling, which Homer, listening, does not betray.

BEAUTY A GIFT OF MIXED BLESSINGS

The exile's lament is the last to echo over Hector's remains; it bathes the end of the *Iliad* in the pure, desolate light of compassion. "This is now the twentieth year from the time I came away and left my native land; yet I have never heard a bad or a harsh word from you. So I weep for you and for my unhappy self too, with grief at heart. I have nobody else now in wide Troy to be kind or gentle to me; everybody shudders away from me." This, however, is not the moan of some humiliated creature at the mercy of her tormentors; it is the

---

HELEN LAMENTS FOR HECTOR

This is the full text of the scene from Book XXIV of the Iliad *in which Helen mourns for the dead Hector.*

Helen followed now and led them [the women mourning for Hector] in a third lament: 'Hector, I loved you far the best of all my Trojan brothers. Prince Paris brought me here and married me (I wish I had perished first), but in all the nineteen years since I came away and left my own country, it is from you that I have never heard a single harsh or spiteful word. Others in the house insulted me—your brothers, your sisters, your brothers' wealthy wives, even your mother, though your father could not be more gentle with me if he were my own. But you protested every time and stopped them, out of the kindness of your heart, in your own courteous way. So these tears of sorrow that I shed are both for you and for my miserable self. No one else is left in the wide realm of Troy to treat me gently and befriend me. They shudder at me as I pass.' Thus Helen through her tears; and the countless multitude wailed with her.

grief of a mortal at the mercy of gods who have laden her with dazzling graces, the better to balk her of the joy these gifts seemed to promise. No matter who wins in the end, Helen, unlike Andromache and the Trojan princesses, does not have to fear a life of slavery and forced labor "under the eyes of a harsh master." After twenty years, she is still the stake the war is being fought for, and the reward the winner will carry off. In the depths of her wretchedness, Helen still wears an air of majesty that keeps the world at a distance and flouts old age and death. The most beautiful of women seemed born for a radiant destiny; everything pointed that way; everything appeared to contribute to it. But, as it turns out, the gods only chose her to work misfortune on herself and on the two nations. Beauty is not a promise of happiness here; it is a burden and a curse. At the same time, it isolates and elevates; it has something preservative in it that wards off outrage and shame. Hence its sacred character—to use the word in its original, ambiguous sense—on the one hand, lifegiving, exalting; on the other, accursed and dread. The Helen the two armies are contending for will never be Paris' any more than she has been Menelaus'; the Trojans cannot own her any more than the Greeks could. Beauty, captured, remains elusive. It deserts alike those who beget, or contemplate, or desire it. Homer endows it with the inexorability of force or fate. Like force, it subjugates and destroys— exalts and releases. It is not by some chance, arising out of her life's vicissitudes, that Helen has come to be the cause of the war and its stake; a deeper necessity has brought her there to join the apparition of beauty with the unleashing of rage. Beside the warriors and above them, Helen is the calm and the bitterness that spring up in the thick of battle, casting their cool shadow over victories and defeats alike, over the living and the thousands of dead. . . .

HELEN NOT TO BLAME

Homer carefully abstains from the description of beauty, as though this might constitute a forbidden anticipation of bliss. The shade of Helen's eyes, of Thetis' tresses, the line of Andromache's shoulders—these details are kept from us. No singularity, no particularity is brought to our notice; yet we see these women; we would recognize them. One wonders by what impalpable means Homer manages to give us such a sense of the plastic reality of his characters. Incorruptible,

Helen's beauty passes from life into the poem, from flesh into marble, its pulse still throbbing. The statue's mouth utters a human cry, and from the empty eyes gush "tender tears." When Helen climbs the ramparts of Troy to watch the fight between Paris and Menelaus, one can almost feel the loftiness of her step. By the Scaean gates, the Trojan elders are holding council. At the sight of her, "the good orators" fall silent, struck to the heart. They cannot help finding her beautiful. And this beauty frightens them like a bad omen, a warning of death. "She has terribly the look, close-up, of the immortal goddesses. . . . But even so, whatever she may be, let her set sail and go away. Let her not be left here to be a scourge to us and our sons hereafter." Here—and this is unusual—the poet himself, speaking through Priam, lifts his voice to exonerate beauty and proclaim it innocent of man's misfortunes. "I do not blame you. I blame the gods, who launched this Achaean war, full of tears, upon me." The real culprits, and the only ones, are the gods, who live "exempt from care," while men are consumed with sorrow. The curse which turns beauty into destructive fatality does not originate in the human heart. The diffuse guilt of Becoming pools into a single sin, the one sin condemned and explicitly stigmatized by Homer: the happy carelessness of the Immortals.

There follows a scene of starry serenity in which the human accent, however, is still audible. Priam asks Helen to tell him the names of the most famous of the Achaean warriors that he can see in the enemy camp. The battlefield is quiet; a few steps away from each other, the two armies stand face to face awaiting the single combat that will decide the outcome of the war. Here, at the very peak of the *Iliad, is* one of those pauses, those moments of contemplation, when the spell of Becoming is broken, and the world of action, with all its fury, dips into peace. The plain where the warrior herd was raging is no more than a tranquil mirage to Helen and the old king. . . .

Meanwhile Helen stands helplessly watching the men who are going to do battle for her. She is there still, since nations that brave each other for markets, for raw materials, rich lands, and their treasures, are fighting, first and forever, for Helen.

Force as the Central Concept of the *Iliad*

Simone Weil

This powerful essay, one of the most famous ever
composed about Homer's epics, is the work of
Simone Weil (1909–1943), a brilliant French-Jewish
philosopher and scholar whose writings consistently
address the subjects of religion and pacifism. Weil
begins with a clever and beautifully apt metaphor
that perfectly sums up her argument, namely that
the *Iliad* is a mirror of life, reflecting the naked,
pitiless element of force that lies at the center of both
the poem and human history. She goes on to suggest
that in human endeavors the strong usually have
little or no regard for the weak; yet the strong are
also inevitably overconfident and so fail to see their
own vulnerability to the ravages of time, nature,
and fate, and in the end the wheel of fate brings ruin
upon them, too.

The true hero, the true subject, the center of the *Iliad* is
force. Force employed by man, force that enslaves man,
force before which man's flesh shrinks away. In this work, at
all times, the human spirit is shown as modified by its relations with force, as swept away, blinded, by the very force it
imagined it could handle, as deformed by the weight of the
force it submits to. For those dreamers who considered that
force, thanks to progress, would soon be a thing of the past,
the *Iliad* could appear as an historical document; for others,
whose powers of recognition are more acute and who perceive force, today as yesterday, at the very center of human
history, the *Iliad* is the purest and the loveliest of mirrors.

To define force—it is that x that turns anybody who is
subjected to it into a *thing*. Exercised to the limit, it turns
man into a thing in the most literal sense: it makes a corpse

Reprinted from The Iliad, *or the Poem of Force* by Simone Weil, translated by Mary
McCarthy (Wallingford, Pa.: Pendle Hill Pamphlets, 1957). © and permission granted
by the Mary McCarthy Literary Trust.

out of him. Somebody was here, and the next minute there is nobody here at all; this is a spectacle the *Iliad* never wearies of showing us:

> . . . the horses
> Rattled the empty chariots through the files of battle,
> Longing for their noble drivers. But they on the ground
> Lay, dearer to the vultures than to their wives.

The hero becomes a *thing* dragged behind a chariot in the dust:

> All around, his black hair
> Was spread; in the dust his whole head lay,
> That once-charming head; now Zeus had let his enemies
> Defile it on his native soil.

The bitterness of such a spectacle is offered us absolutely undiluted. No comforting fiction intervenes; no consoling prospect of immortality; and on the hero's head no washed-out halo of patriotism descends. . . . Still more poignant—so painful is the contrast—is the sudden evocation, as quickly rubbed out, of another world: the faraway, precarious, touching world of peace, of the family, the world in which each man counts more than anything else to those about him.

> She ordered her bright-haired maids in the palace
> To place on the fire a large tripod, preparing
> A hot bath for Hector, returning from battle.
> Foolish woman! Already he lay, far from hot baths,
> Slain by grey-eyed Athena, who guided Achilles' arm.

Far from hot baths he was indeed, poor man. And not he alone. Nearly all the *Iliad* takes place far from hot baths. Nearly all of human life, then and now, takes place far from hot baths.

Here we see force in its grossest and most summary form—the force that kills. How much more varied in its processes, how much more surprising in its effects is the other force, the force that does *not* kill, i.e., that does not kill just yet. It will surely kill, it will possibly kill, or perhaps it merely hangs, poised and ready, over the head of the creature it *can* kill, at any moment, which is to say at every moment. In whatever aspect, its effect is the same: it turns a man into a stone. From its first property (the ability to turn a human being into a thing by the simple method of killing him) flows another, quite prodigious too in its own way, the ability to turn a human being into a thing while he is still alive. . . .

A man stands disarmed and naked with a weapon pointing at him; this person becomes a corpse before anybody or
anything touches him. Just a minute ago, he was thinking,
acting, hoping. . . . Soon, however, he grasps the fact that the
weapon which is pointing at him will not be diverted; and
now, still breathing, he is simply matter; still thinking, he
can think no longer:

> Thus spoke the brilliant son of Priam
> In begging words. But he heard a harsh reply:
> He spoke. And the other's knees and heart failed him.
> Dropping his spear, he knelt down, holding out his arms.
> Achilles, drawing his sharp sword, struck
> Through the neck and breastbone. The two-edged sword
> Sunk home its full length. The other, face down,
> Lay still, and the black blood ran out, wetting the ground . . .

NO SHIELD AGAINST TEARS

Perhaps all men, by the very act of being born, are destined
to suffer violence; yet this is a truth to which circumstance
shuts men's eyes. The strong are, as a matter of fact, never absolutely strong, nor are the weak absolutely weak, but neither is aware of this. They have in common a refusal to believe that they both belong to the same species: the weak see
no relation between themselves and the strong, and vice
versa. The man who is the possessor of force seems to walk
through a non-resistant element; in the human substance
that surrounds him nothing has the power to interpose, between the impulse and the act, the tiny interval that is reflection. Where there is no room for reflection, there is none either for justice or prudence. Hence we see men in arms
behaving harshly and madly. We see their sword bury itself
in the breast of a disarmed enemy who is in the very act of
pleading at their knees. We see them triumph over a dying
man by describing to him the outrages his corpse will endure. We see Achilles cut the throats of twelve Trojan boys on
the funeral pyre of Patroclus as naturally as we cut flowers
for a grave. These men, wielding power, have no suspicion of
the fact that the consequences of their deeds will at length
come home to them—they too will bow the neck in their
turn. . . . Achilles rejoices over the sight of the Greeks fleeing
in misery and confusion. What could possibly suggest to him
that this rout, which will last exactly as long as he wants it to
and end when his mood indicates it, that this very rout will
be the cause of his friend's death, and, for that matter, of his

own? Thus it happens that those who have force on loan from fate count on it too much and are destroyed.

But at the time their own destruction seems impossible to them. For they do not see that the force in their possession is only a limited quantity; nor do they see their relations with other human beings as a kind of balance between unequal amounts of force. Since other people do not impose on their movements that halt, that interval of hesitation, wherein lies all our consideration for our brothers in humanity, they conclude that destiny has given complete license to them, and none at all to their inferiors. And at this point they exceed the measure of the force that is actually at their disposal. Inevitably they exceed it, since they are not aware that it is limited. And now we see them committed irretrievably to chance; suddenly things cease to obey them. Sometimes chance is kind to them, sometimes cruel. But in any case there they are, exposed, open to misfortune; gone is the armor of power that formerly protected their naked souls; nothing, no shields, stands between them and tears.

This retribution, which has a geometrical rigor, which operates automatically to penalize the abuse of force, was the main subject of Greek thought. It is the soul of the epic. Under the name of Nemesis, it functions as the mainspring of Aeschylus's tragedies. To the Pythagoreans, to Socrates and Plato [a succession of Greek philosophers], it was the jumping-off point of speculation upon the nature of man and the universe. Wherever Hellenism [Greek culture] has penetrated, we find the idea of it familiar. In Oriental [Eastern] countries which are steeped in Buddhism, it is perhaps this Greek idea that has lived on under the name of Kharma. The Occident [Western world], however, has lost it, and no longer even has a word to express it in any of its languages: conceptions of limit, measure, equilibrium, which ought to determine the conduct of life are, in the West, restricted to a servile function in the vocabulary of technics. We are only geometricians of matter; the Greeks were, first of all, geometricians in their apprenticeship to virtue.

WORDS OF REASON DISREGARDED

Thus violence obliterates anybody who feels its touch. It comes to seem just as external to its employer as to its victim. And from this springs the idea of a destiny before which executioner and victim stand equally innocent, before which conquered and conqueror are brothers in the same distress. The conquered brings misfortune to the conqueror, and vice versa: "A single son, short-lived, was born to him. / Neglected by me, he grows old—for far from home / I camp before Troy, injuring you and your sons."

A One-Sided Interpretation

Many scholars feel that though masterfully expressed Weil's argument fails to take into account certain realities about Homeric society, as shown in these critical comments by scholar Seth L. Schein in his book The Mortal Hero.

Weil fully appreciates the sheer physicality of the poem's descriptions of killing, dying, and supplicating for life. She does sensitive and eloquent justice to the pathos and poignancy of war and death in the *Iliad*, illuminating Homer's portrayal of the individual and social cost of heroism. But her interpretation is one-sided and fails to recognize the nobility and glory of the slayers along with the humanity and pathos of the slain. Weil makes this omission because, like others who read the *Iliad* as an antiwar poem, she tacitly substitutes for its social and cultural values her own spiritual categories.

Weil views the *Iliad* through Christian lenses. She sees force in the poem as exercising tyranny "over the soul," which "enslaved to war cries out for deliverance"; however, as has been pointed out, such a concept of the "soul" does not exist in the Homeric universe. . . . These flaws in Weil's argument are grounded not in the poem but in her view of life. Her interpretation is beautifully expressed and makes sense in the light of her own spirituality and of [her reactions as a Jew to] Nazi violence [during World War II]; it is not, however, an accurate reading of the poem. We inevitably distort and misread the *Iliad* when we foist the values of another time and culture upon its objective, internally consistent presentation of and attitude toward war and death.

A moderate use of force, which alone would enable man to escape being enmeshed in its machinery, would require superhuman virtue, which is as rare as dignity in weakness. Moreover, moderation itself is not without its perils, since prestige, from which force derives at least three quarters of its strength, rests principally upon that marvelous indifference that the strong feel toward the weak, an indifference so contagious that it infects the very people who are the objects of it. Yet ordinarily excess is not arrived at through prudence or politic considerations. On the contrary, man dashes to it as to an irresistible temptation. The voice of reason is occasionally heard in the mouths of the characters in the *Iliad.* Thersites' speeches are reasonable to the highest degree; so are the speeches of the angry Achilles:

> Nothing is worth my life, not all the goods
> They say the well-built city of Ilium contains. . . .
> A man can capture steers and fatted sheep
> But, once gone, the soul cannot be captured back.

But words of reason drop into the void. If they come from an inferior, he is punished and shuts up; if from a chief, his actions betray them. And failing everything else, there is always a god handy to advise him to be unreasonable. In the end, the very idea of wanting to escape the role fate has allotted one—the business of killing and dying—disappears from the mind. . . .

MOMENTS OF GRACE AND LOVE

The wantonness of the conqueror that knows no respect for any creature or thing that is at its mercy or is imagined to be so, the despair of the soldier that drives him on to destruction, the obliteration of the slave or the conquered man, the wholesale slaughter—all these elements combine in the *Iliad* to make a picture of uniform horror, of which force is the sole hero. A monotonous desolation would result were it not for those few luminous moments, scattered here and there throughout the poem, those brief, celestial moments in which man possesses his soul. The soul that awakes then, to live for an instant only and be lost almost at once in force's vast kingdom, awakes pure and whole; it contains no ambiguities, nothing complicated or turbid; it has no room for anything but courage and love. Sometimes it is in the course of inner deliberations that a man finds his soul: he meets it, like Hector before Troy, as he tries to face destiny on his own terms, without the help of gods or men. At other times, it is in a moment of love that men discover their souls—and there is hardly any form of pure love known to humanity of which the *Iliad* does not treat. The tradition of hospitality persists, even through several generations, to dispel the blindness of combat.

> Thus I am for you a beloved guest in the breast of Argos . . .
> Let us turn our lances away from each other, even in battle.

The love of the son for the parents, of father for son, of mother for son, is continually described, in a manner as touching as it is curt: "Thetis answered, shedding tears, / 'You were born to me for a short life, my child, as you say. . . .'" Even brotherly love: "My three brothers whom the same mother bore for me, / So dear.". . . The most beautiful friendship of all, the friendship between comrades-at-arms, is the final theme of The Epic: ". . . But Achilles / Wept, dreaming of the beloved comrade; sleep, all-prevailing, / Would not take him; he turned over again and again." But the purest triumph of love, the crowning grace of war, is the friendship that floods the hearts of mortal enemies. Before it a murdered son or a murdered friend no longer cries out for vengeance. Before it—even more miraculous—the distance between benefactor and suppliant, between victor and vanquished, shrinks to nothing:

> But when thirst and hunger had been appeased,
> Then Dardanian Priam fell to admiring Achilles.
> How tall he was, and handsome; he had the face of a god;
> And in his turn Dardanian Priam was admired by Achilles,
> Who watched his handsome face and listened to his words.
> And when they were satisfied with contemplation of each
>   other . . .

These moments of grace are rare in the *Iliad*, but they are enough to make us feel with sharp regret what it is that violence has killed and will kill again. . . .

WITHOUT MISERY, NO JUSTICE

In any case, this poem is a miracle. Its bitterness is the only justifiable bitterness, for it springs from the subjections of the human spirit to force, that is, in the last analysis, to matter. This subjection is the common lot, although each spirit will bear it differently, in proportion to its own virtue. No one in the *Iliad* is spared by it, as no one on earth is. No one who succumbs to it is by virtue of this fact regarded with contempt. Whoever, within his own soul and in human relations, escapes the dominion of force is loved but loved sorrowfully because of the threat of destruction that constantly hangs over him.

Such is the spirit of the only true epic the Occident possesses. The *Odyssey* seems merely a good imitation, now of the *Iliad*, now of Oriental poems; the *Aeneid* [the epic poem by the first-century B.C. Roman writer Virgil] is an imitation which, however brilliant, is disfigured by frigidity, bombast, and bad taste. . . .

Attic [Athenian] tragedy, or at any rate the tragedy of Aeschylus and Sophocles, is the true continuation of the epic. The conception of justice enlightens it, without ever directly intervening in it; here force appears in its coldness and hardness, always attended by effects from whose fatality neither those who use it nor those who suffer it can escape; here the shame of the coerced spirit is neither disguised, nor enveloped in facile pity, nor held up to scorn; here more than one spirit bruised and degraded by misfortune is offered for our admiration. The Gospels are the last marvelous expression of the Greek genius, as the *Iliad* is the first: here the Greek spirit reveals itself not only in the injunction given mankind to seek above all other goods, "the kingdom and justice of our Heavenly Father," but also in the fact that human suffering is laid bare, and we see it in a being who is at once divine and human. The accounts of the Passion show that a divine spirit, incarnate, is changed by misfortune, trembles before suffering and death, feels itself, in the depths of its agony, to be cut off from man and God. The sense of human misery gives the Gospels that accent of simplicity that is the mark of the Greek genius, and that endows Greek tragedy and the *Iliad* with all their value. . . . This accent cannot be separated from the idea that inspired the Gospels, for the sense of human misery is a pre-condition of justice and love. He who does not realize to what extent shifting fortune and necessity hold in subjection every human spirit, cannot regard as fellow-creatures nor love as he loves himself those whom chance separated from him by an abyss. The variety of constraints pressing upon man give rise to the illusion of several distinct species that cannot communicate. Only he who has measured the dominion of force, and knows how not to respect it, is capable of love and justice.

CHAPTER 3

The *Odyssey*: Its Text, Themes, and Characters

READINGS ON

HOMER

The Story Told in the *Odyssey*

Mark P.O. Morford and Robert J. Lenardon

Here, from their widely respected book *Classical
Mythology*, scholars Mark P.O. Morford of the
University of Virginia and Robert J. Lenardon of
Ohio State University offer a brief summary of the
main events of Homer's *Odyssey*. Almost but not
quite a direct sequel to the *Iliad* (which does not
describe the fall of Troy, the event immediately
preceding the opening of the *Odyssey*), this is the
story of a wise and good man who, by kindling the
wrath of the god Poseidon, is forced to wander for
ten years and endure many hardships before finally
laying eyes once more on his beloved homeland, the
island of Ithaca.

The return of Odysseus forms a saga in itself, to which many
folk tale elements have accrued. Here is Aristotle's summary
of the *Odyssey:* "The story of the *Odyssey* is not long; a man
is away from home for many years; Poseidon constantly is
on the watch to destroy him, and he is alone; at home his
property is being wasted by suitors, and his son is the intended victim of a plot. He reaches home, tempest-tossed; he
makes himself known, attacks his enemies and destroys
them, and is himself saved. This is the heart of the matter:
the rest is episodes" *(Poetics 17)*. The most interesting part of
the legend, however, lies in the "episodes" that comprise
Odysseus' adventures on his travels . . . usually escaping
from danger through his intelligence and courage. He meets
with many men and women, with goddesses and monsters,
and he remains faithful, even after twenty years, to the vision of Penelope, the wife whom he left in Ithaca with his
son, Telemachus. The poet begins in the middle of Odysseus'
adventures, with the hero detained (not unpleasantly, it

Reprinted from *Classical Mythology* by Mark P.O. Morford and Robert J. Lenardon, 3rd
ed. ©1985 by Longman, Inc. Reprinted by permission of Addison-Wesley Educational
Publishers Inc.

would seem) on Ogygia, the island of the nymph Calypso. It is after he has sailed away from the island and his raft has been wrecked that Odysseus relates to his rescuers the events previous to his arrival on Ogygia. After this "flashback," the poem continues with the arrival of Odysseus on Ithaca, his revenge on the suitors for the hand of Penelope, and his eventual recognition by and reunion with Penelope. The resourceful character of Odysseus dominates the story, but it should be noted that the gods also play a significant part, especially Poseidon, who is hostile to the hero, and Athena, his protectress. The hero and his adventures are best introduced by Homer himself in the opening lines (1–21) of the *Odyssey:*

> Of the man tell me, O Muse, the man of many ways, who traveled afar after he had sacked the holy city of Troy. He experienced the cities and the thoughts of many men, and his spirit suffered many sorrows on the sea, as he labored for his own life and for the homecoming of his companions. Yet even so he could not protect his companions, much though he wished it, for they perished by their own folly. . . .

> This man alone, longing for his homecoming and his wife, did the nymph, the lady Calypso, keep in her hollow cave, desiring him as her husband. But when, as the years rolled round, that year came in which the gods had destined his return home to Ithaca, not even then did he escape from his labors nor was he with his friends. Yet the gods pitied him, all except Poseidon, and he unrelentingly was hostile to godlike Odysseus, until he returned to his own land.

THE CAVE OF THE CYCLOPS

It took Odysseus ten years to reach home. When he and his contingent left Troy their first landfall was the Thracian city of Ismarus, home of the Cicones; after sacking it Odysseus and his men were driven off by other Cicones who attacked them as they were enjoying the booty from the city. The Greeks had spared Maron, priest of Apollo, in their attack, and he in return gave them among other presents twelve jars of fragrant red wine, which was to prove its value later. As they sailed away they were driven southward by a violent storm and eventually came to the land of the lotus eaters; here their reception was friendly but no less dangerous, for he who ate of the fruit of the lotus forgot everything and wanted only to stay where he was, eating lotus fruit. Odysseus got his men away, even those who had tasted the fruit, and sailed to the land of the Cyclopes.

The Cyclopes were one-eyed giants, herdsmen, living each in his own cave. One of them was Polyphemus, son of Poseidon, and it was his cave that Odysseus and twelve picked companions entered as they explored the area. Polyphemus was out, and in the cave were sheep and lambs, cheeses, and other provisions; the Greeks helped themselves to these and waited for the return of the cave's owner. In the evening Polyphemus returned with his flocks, shut the entrance of the cave with a huge stone, and then caught sight of the visitors, two of whom he ate for his supper; he breakfasted on two more the next day and another two when he returned the second evening. Now Odysseus had with him some of the wine of Maron, and with this he made Polyphemus drunk; he told him his name was Nobody and the giant in return for the excellent wine promised that he would reward Nobody by eating him last. He then fell asleep, and Odysseus took his revenge. He sharpened a wooden stake that was lying in the cave and heated it in the fire; then he and his surviving men drove it into the solitary eye of the sleeping giant. As he cried out in agony the other Cyclopes came running to the cave's entrance, only to hear the cry "Nobody is killing me," so that they assumed that not much was wrong and left Polyphemus alone. Next morning Polyphemus, now blind, removed the stone at the entrance and let his flocks out; he felt each animal as it passed him. But Odysseus had tied his men each to the undersides of three sheep, and himself clung to the belly of the biggest ram; so he and his men escaped. As Odysseus sailed away in his ship he shouted his real name to the Cyclops, who hurled the top of a mountain at him and nearly wrecked the ship. Polyphemus had long before been warned of Odysseus by a prophet, and as he recognized the name he prayed to his father Poseidon:

> Grant that Odysseus may not return home, but if it is fated for him once more to see those he loves and reach his home and country, then let him arrive after many years, in distress, without his companions, upon another's ship—and may he find trouble in his house.

MEN TRANSFORMED INTO SWINE

The prayer was heard. Odysseus, now reunited with the rest of his fleet, next reached the floating island of Aeolus, keeper of the winds, who lived there with his six sons, who were married to his six daughters. After he had entertained Odysseus, Aeolus gave him as a parting gift a leather bag containing all the winds, and showed him which one to release so as to reach home. Thus he sailed back to Ithaca and was within reach of land when he fell asleep; his men, believing that the bag contained gold that Odysseus was keeping for himself, opened it, and all the winds rushed out and blew the ships back to Aeolus' island. Aeolus refused to help them any more, for, he supposed, they must be hated by the gods.

Accordingly they sailed away, this time to the land of the Laestrygonians, who were cannibals; they sank all Odysseus' ships except his own and ate up the crews. So Polyphemus' curse was already working, and Odysseus sailed on with his solitary ship to the island of Aeaea, the home of the witch Circe.... Odysseus divided his men into two groups; he stayed behind with the one while the other, twenty-three men in all, went to visit the ruler of the island. They found Circe with various animals around her, and themselves (except for one, Eurylochus, who brought the news back to Odysseus) were turned, by eating her food, into pigs—swine in appearance and sound, but still with human minds. As Odysseus went to rescue his men he was met by the god Hermes, who told him how to counter Circe's charms and gave him as an antidote the magic herb *moly*, whose "root is black and flower as white as milk." So he ate Circe's food unharmed; as she tried to transform him into a pig he threatened her with his sword and made her change his men back into their human shape. Odysseus lived with Circe for a year and by her begot a son, Telegonus.

CIRCE'S PROPHECY

At the end of a year Odysseus, urged on by his men, asked Circe to send him on his way home. She agreed, but told him that he first had to go to the Underworld and there learn the way home from Tiresias, whose prophetic powers were unimpaired even in the world of the dead. The visit of Odysseus to the Underworld ... is in some ways the climax of his adventures, for the conquest of death is the most formidable struggle a hero has to face.... Following Circe's directions, [Odysseus] sailed with his men to the River of Ocean at the western limit of the world.... Here was the entrance to the world of the dead and Odysseus, alone, performed his ritual. Many ghosts came, most important of whom was the soul of Tiresias, who told Odysseus of the disasters that yet waited for him on his journey; he would reach home, but alone and after many years (in this Tiresias echoes the prayer of Polyphemus)....

Circe sent him on his way after warning him of the dangers that lay ahead. First were the Sirens (said by Homer to be two in number, but to be more by other authors); to Homer these were human in form, but in popular tradition they were birdlike, with women's heads. From their island meadow they would lure passing sailors onto the rocks; all around them were the whitened bones of their victims. Odysseus sailed by them unharmed, stopping his men's ears with wax, while he had himself bound to the ship's mast so that he could not yield to the irresistible beauty of the Sirens' song....

Circe [also] told Odysseus of the island of Thrinacia, where Helius (the Sun) pastured his herds of cattle and sheep; she strictly warned Odysseus not to touch a single one of the animals if he and his men wished ever to return to Ithaca. But Odysseus' men in the event could not show such restraint after weeks of being detained by adverse winds, and while he was sleeping they killed some of the cattle for food. Helius complained to Zeus, and as a punishment (for the sacrilege of killing the god's cattle) Zeus raised a storm when the ship set sail and hurled a thunderbolt at it. The ship sank, and all the men were drowned except for Odysseus, who escaped, floating on the mast and part of the keel.

CALYPSO AND NAUSICAA

So much for Circe's prophecy and the subsequent events. After the wreck Odysseus drifted ... over the sea to Ogygia, the island home of Calypso, daughter of Atlas. It is at this stage in his adventures that Odysseus' part in the *Odyssey* begins.

He lived with Calypso for seven years; although she loved him and offered to make him immortal, he could not forget Penelope. Finally, after Hermes brought her the express orders of Zeus, Calypso helped Odysseus build a raft and sail away. Even now he was not free from disaster; Poseidon saw him as he approached Scheria (the island of the Phaeacians) and shattered the raft with a storm. Odysseus was in the water for two days and two nights, but he survived ... and he succeeded in reaching land naked, exhausted, and alone.

The king of the Phaeacians was Alcinous, and his daughter was Nausicaa. The very day after Odysseus' landing Nau-

sicaa went to wash clothes near the seashore and came face
to face with Odysseus; she gave him her protection and
brought him back to the palace. Here he was warmly entertained by Alcinous and his queen, Arete, and related the story
of his adventures to them. The Phaeacians gave him rich gifts
and a day later brought him back to Ithaca in a deep sleep on
one of their ships (they were magnificent seamen). So
Odysseus reached Ithaca ten years after the fall of Troy, alone
and on another's ship, as Polyphemus had prayed. . . .

DISGUISED AS A BEGGAR

In Ithaca more than one hundred suitors—young noblemen
from Ithaca and the nearby islands—were courting Penelope
in the hope of taking Odysseus' place as her husband and as
king of Ithaca (for Telemachus, Odysseus' son by Penelope,
was considered still too young to succeed). They spent their
days feasting at Odysseus' palace, wasting his possessions.
Penelope, however, remained faithful to Odysseus, even
though he seemed to be dead; she procrastinated with the
suitors by promising to choose one of them when she should
have finished weaving a magnificent cloak to be a burial
garment for Odysseus' father, Laertes. For three years she
wove the robe by day and undid her work by night, but in the
fourth year her deception was uncovered and a decision was
now unavoidable. It was at this stage that Odysseus returned; helped by Athena, he gained entrance at the palace
disguised as a beggar, after being recognized by his faithful
old swineherd, Eumaeus, and by Telemachus. . . . (It was
outside the palace that Odysseus' old hound, Argus, recognized his master after nineteen years' absence, and died.) At
the palace Odysseus was insulted by the suitors and by another beggar, Irus, whom he knocked out in a fight. Still in
disguise, he had a long talk with Penelope, in which he gave
an exact description of Odysseus and of a curious brooch he
had worn; as a result she confided in him her plan to give
herself next day to whichever suitor should succeed in
stringing Odysseus' great bow and shooting an arrow
straight through a row of twelve ax heads. . . .

The trial of the bow took place next day; none of the suitors could even so much as string it, and Odysseus asked to
be allowed to try. Effortlessly he achieved the task and shot
the arrow through the axes; next he shot the leading suitor,
Antinous, and in the succeeding fight he and Telemachus

and their two faithful servants killed all the other suitors. . . .

After the suitors had all been killed, Odysseus cleansed the hall and hanged the twelve maidservants who had allowed themselves to be seduced by the suitors. Even so, Penelope could not believe it really was Odysseus who was there, and only when he showed knowledge of the secret construction of their bed did she relent and end their twenty years' separation. . . .

The next day Odysseus made himself known to his father, Laertes; the *Odyssey* ends with Athena intervening between Odysseus and the relatives of the dead suitors (who demanded vengeance, blood for blood) and making peace between them.

How the *Odyssey* Differs in Shape and Character from the *Iliad*

C.M. Bowra

Since ancient times, scholars have remarked on the differences in style and spirit between the two epic poems traditionally attributed to Homer. This has led some to speculate that the works were composed by different authors; however, a majority of modern scholars tentatively accept the single author thesis, proposing that the *Odyssey*'s generally less heroic, more lifelike tone reflects changes in Homer's style due to his advancing years, the more passionate *Iliad* being a work of his youth. This essay, by the highly respected classical scholar C.M. Bowra, former vice-chancellor of Oxford University, focuses on the shape and character of the *Odyssey*, exploring the differences, as well as some of the similarities and connections, between it and Homer's earlier epic.

The *Odyssey*, like the *Iliad*, begins with an invocation to the Muse:

> Tell, Muse, of the man of many devices, who wandered far indeed, when he had sacked the holy citadel of Troy. He saw the cities of many men and knew their minds, and many were the sorrows which he suffered in his spirit on the sea, when he tried to win his own life and the return of his companions. But not even so, for all his desire, did he save his companions; for they were destroyed by their own insolence, when they ate the cattle of the Sun Hyperion; and he robbed them of the day of their return. From what point you will, goddess, daughter of Zeus, speak to us also.

This presents several surprises. Unlike Achilles at the start of the *Iliad*, the hero of the *Odyssey* is not named but called 'the man of many devices', which indicates that his story is familiar, and this is confirmed by the last words when the

Muse is asked to 'speak to us also'. But the familiar story is outlined in a peculiar way. The fantastic adventures of Odysseus are inadequately, almost deceptively, suggested in the reference to cities and minds; almost the only city seen by him is the capital of Phaeacia, and minds are not what he marks in the Cyclops and other monsters. Next, the emphasis on his struggle to save his own life is fair enough and anticipates some of his bravest efforts, but he hardly does so much to secure the return of his comrades. He looks after them, but he takes risks with their lives, and more than once he is the cause of their loss. Finally, not a word is said about the Suitors and the vengeance on them. They occupy more than half the poem and provide its central theme. The opening lines of the *Odyssey* are much less apt and less relevant than those of the *Iliad*. . . .

A SEQUEL TO THE *ILIAD*

The material of the *Odyssey* differs greatly from that of the *Iliad* and gives it a different character. While the *Iliad* tells of the 'glorious doings of men' and is heroic in the sense that heroes struggle against other heroes, the *Odyssey* uses a less specific and less exalted material. Its stories are ultimately fairy-tales or folktales, and are unheroic in the sense that the unquestionable hero Odysseus is faced not by his equals but by his inferiors or by monsters. In its own compass it displays two kinds of narrative. Books 1–4 and 13–24 tell the age-old tale of the Wanderer's Return and his vengeance on the Suitors who devour his substance and try to marry his wife. In this there is not much fantasy or marvel. . . . The two parts differ greatly in matter, scale, temper and outlook. The second consists of stories so ancient that they seem to have been polished and perfected by constant telling, while the first class, which deals with stories hardly less ancient but of a different kind, has a less confident and less accomplished, even more experimental and more tentative, air.

The *Odyssey* serves in some sense as a sequel to the *Iliad*. No doubt there were many such sequels, especially in the creative heyday of oral song. The tale of Troy had many consequences, and among these were the adventures of Odysseus. In time he became the chief of the surviving heroes, and his return the most famous of many. Once a figure becomes known for certain qualities, appropriate adventures, with which he may originally have had no connexion, are attached to him and marked with his personal imprint. Odysseus seems from the start to have been 'wily' and 'much-enduring', and stories which turned on wiliness or endurance were annexed to him. The relation of the *Odyssey* to the *Iliad* is obvious throughout. The past in retrospect is seen to have been disastrous, the story of 'evil Ilium not to be named', words which do not occur in the *Iliad* and suggest a shift of attitude towards the Trojan War. At the start of the *Odyssey*, when the gods discuss the fate of Odysseus as he languishes on Calypso's island, they turn at once to the fate of his old comrade, Agamemnon, who has been murdered by his wife and her lover, and this broaches the topic of what happens to the heroes of Troy. The audience knows all about the Trojan War and can take any reference to it. So now it lies in the background as they hear about Odysseus and Ithaca.

FAMILIAR CHARACTERS REAPPEAR

In the *Odyssey* certain characters appear who have played a substantial part in the *Iliad* but need not necessarily play any part in the return of Odysseus. When Telemachus sails off to find news of his father, he visits first Nestor at Pylos and then Menelaus and Helen at Sparta. Nestor is just the same as in the *Iliad*, garrulous, generous, helpful, even wise. Actually he contributes very little to Telemachus' knowledge of his father, and Homer shows a flicker of playful malice when Telemachus, eager to embark on his ship at Pylos and get home, decides to do so without seeing Nestor, since this would waste a lot of time, and sends the young Peisistratus to fix things with him. Menelaus is a less marked personality than Nestor, but he shows the kingly qualities which we expect from him, and especially loyalty to the son of his old friend Odysseus. More striking is Helen, who makes only a few appearances in the *Iliad* but in all of them reveals the pathos of her doom and her desire to escape from it. Her capacity for affection is clear from what she says to Priam, to Hector in his lifetime, and about him after his death. The whole adventure with Paris has been a sorrow and a disaster for her, but she has not been able to avoid it. Now she is back with Menelaus at Sparta, happy and at peace. She recalls without distress episodes from the war, but the scope of her character is revealed when she sees that Menelaus and his guests are distressing themselves with reminiscences, and mixes a drug which she has brought from Egypt and which deadens pain and sorrow. She has learned from her sufferings, and the tenderness which is already hers in the *Iliad is* turned to new purposes.

Odysseus himself in the *Odyssey* is an enlarged and elaborated version of what he is in the *Iliad*. His main qualities there are cunning and endurance. He keeps his head when others lose theirs, notably after Agamemnon's ill-judged test of the army's morale. He is throughout a notable leader, resourceful and brave. In the *Odyssey*, where he is far longer on the stage, some of his qualities are turned in new directions. First, his cunning is tested in unfamiliar conditions, as in the cave of the Cyclops, where he takes on some qualities of a folk-hero and sustains them quite convincingly. Secondly, his need for cunning is enforced by his own recklessness. It is his fault that he is trapped in the cave of the Cyclops, since he has insisted on entering it, and equally it is his fault that he seeks out Circe's dwelling by himself. Thirdly, his abundant appetites, known from his taste for food and drink in the *Iliad*, are extended in the *Odyssey* to living with Circe and with Calypso, not perhaps in entire satisfaction but still competently. Lastly, the warrior of the *Iliad* becomes the returned wanderer of the *Odyssey* and needs all his powers of decision, command and improvisation. These he amply displays. . . . Odysseus in the *Odyssey* is a magnified version of Odysseus in the *Iliad*, but he remains substantially the same man and recognizable in his main being.

A FINAL CURTAIN FOR THE HEROIC AGE

Finally, there are in the *Odyssey* two passages where Homer presents ghosts of the dead, and each includes some chief figures of the *Iliad*. At 11.385–567 Odysseus, at the end of the world, summons ghosts with an offering of blood, and among those who appear are Agamemnon, Achilles and Aias. All three have died since the end of the *Iliad*. Agamemnon has been murdered by his wife, in marked contrast with Odysseus, whose faithful Penelope holds out bravely against the Suitors. His story emphasizes the dangers that await those who return from Troy, but sheds no new light on his personality. Aias, in a brief appearance, adds a new dimension to his simple character in the *Iliad*, for in the interval he has killed himself because his honour has been wounded by Odysseus. Odysseus does his best to appease him, but Aias takes no notice and makes no answer. The most striking figure is Achilles, for his words complement by contrast what he says in Book ix when momentarily he rejects the heroic life. Now he knows what he has lost, for he would rather 'work on the land as the serf of a man with no property, with no great means of life, than reign over all the perished dead'. His only consolation is to know that his son Neoptolemus is already a stout warrior. These three ghosts form a link with the *Iliad,* and when Odysseus speaks to them he speaks to his peers, as he does nowhere else in the *Odyssey.*

More mysterious is 24.1–204, where the ghosts of the Suitors are escorted by Hermes to the land of the dead and met by some heroes of the *Iliad,* notably Achilles and Agamemnon. Though the passage is thought to be a later addition, at least it has a part in the whole plan of the *Odyssey.* Achilles hears of his own death and funeral from Agamemnon; at it the Muses sang and the ceremony is a fitting climax to a heroic life. To this the Suitors present a complete antithesis. Their ignominious deaths are the proper end to their squalid careers. In this passage the poet seems to have aimed at more than one effect. First, when he makes Agamemnon say that Odysseus is indeed fortunate to have a wife like Penelope and very unlike Clytaemnestra, he emphasizes a subsidiary theme of the *Odyssey,* but does not gain much by it. Secondly, the parade of the ghosts of Troy, in which Patroclus, Aias and Antilochus are named as well as Achilles and Agamemnon, provides a final curtain for great figures of the *Iliad* and of the heroic age. Their place here recalls them at the end of a long story, and the renewed attention paid to them brings various themes together in a last bow. Thirdly, there is a real contrast between the death and glory of Achilles, immortalized in song, and the miserable careers of the Suitors, who are at the other extreme from the true nobility of the heroic ideal. Whoever composed this passage, must have felt that the *Odyssey* must be brought into contact with the *Iliad,* and this he did by stressing what real heroes are. . . .

HOMERIC MONSTERS

The sources of the *Odyssey* are different from those of the *Iliad* and the difference explains some of its character. If it deals with marvels and monsters, so to a smaller extent does the *Iliad.* In both poems gods interfere with the course of nature. When Aphrodite spirits Paris away from the battlefield or protects Aeneas, it is not very different from when Athene covers Odysseus with a mist in Phaeacia or changes his appearance to prevent him being recognized. Though the *Iliad* contains the remarkable scene when the horse of Achilles speaks to him, it is because Hera has for this one occasion given it a human voice, and this is well within the power of the gods. The *Odyssey* differs when its marvels are not caused by the gods but belong to the world of legend. The wind-bag of Aeolus, the transformations of Circe, the summoning of ghosts at the end of the world, the monstrosity of Scylla, are outside human experience and do not belong to the strictly heroic world of the *Iliad.* In face of them Odysseus conducts himself heroically, as when he insists on hearing the Sirens' song but forestalls disaster by getting himself lashed to the mast. But the monsters which he has to face are outside both human and heroic experience.

Homer evidently saw this and tried to bring his monsters as near as possible to humanity, to relate them to it, and even in some degree to humanize them. This is certainly the case with the Cyclops, who despite his single eye, his bulk 'like a wooded peak of tall mountains', and his cannibalistic gluttony, is made real by his pastoral life, by his care for his flocks, by his affection for his ram. He is hideous and horrible, but not outside comprehension. Comparable in some respects to him is the queen of the Laestrygonians. She lives in a rocky fjord, and all looks easy until the scouts of Odysseus entering her palace, 'saw a woman as big as a mountain-peak, and they hated her'. She grabs one of them and plans to make her supper of him. She is of the same loathsome breed as the Cyclops, but since he has recently received full treatment, she is deftly conveyed in a short sketch. The Sirens, despite their gift of song which lures men to death and the bones of decaying bodies round them are careful to do no more than invite Odysseus to listen to them on the latest subjects of song. The exception to this realism is Scylla, who is a monster among monsters, aptly and fully described, with her twelve feet, her six necks, each with a head and three rows of teeth; she seizes six men from the ship of Odysseus and eats them while they are still crying for help and stretching out their hands, so that Odysseus comments:

> That was the most piteous thing that I saw with my eyes of all
> that I suffered searching out the ways of the sea.

Scylla must be descended from tales of sea-monsters, of giant krakens and man-slaying cuttle-fish, and perhaps because she has some basis in fact Homer feels that he must describe her exactly. She is far from ordinary, and yet one small touch brings her into the compass of living things—her voice is like that of a puppy. It is quite unexpected and almost absurd, and it is just this that brings it home. The monsters of the *Odyssey* are clearly visualized. Their horror comes not from vagueness but from clearly imagined actions and the menace of a horrible death which they offer. The only approximation to them in the *Iliad is* the Chimaera:

> It was a divine creature, not of human race, in front a lion, in the rear a snake, and in the middle a goat, and it breathed the terrible strength of flaming fire.

Description is reduced to the barest essentials, but the Chimaera emerges clearly. This is the Homeric way of looking at monsters, and it is fully developed in the *Odyssey.* It is quite different from the shapeless horrors which the long northern night gives to its dragons.

REALISM

This controlling realism informs most parts of the *Odyssey* and gives much of its special flavour. It accounts for a certain quiet poetry which is not very noticeable in the *Iliad,* but makes the *Odyssey* friendly and familiar. It finds poetry in quite unassuming and humble subjects, as when Telemachus goes to bed and Euryclea folds his clothes and hangs them on a peg, or his ship sets out in the evening and the wind fills the sail and the dark waves resound about the stern. Life in the palace, despite the disruption caused by the Suitors, follows a routine, and there is a quiet dignity in the reception of guests, the laying out of tables, the scrubbing of them with sponges. In making his raft Odysseus shows a high technical accomplishment, and the mere making has its own interest....

The same kind of realism can be seen in the characters. We have marked how Odysseus is developed from his old self in the *Iliad,* but he is the only character of any complexity, and that is because legend insisted upon a more than common personality. The others go their own way, and make their individual mark. At the start Telemachus is only a boy, and conscious of it. But he wishes to assert himself, even though he lacks the authority and the experience to do so. His voyage to Pylos makes a man of him. On it he settles his own decisions, and, when he comes back to Ithaca, he is ready for action, and follows and helps his father. Penelope presents rather a special problem. Legend marked her as prudent, and she has kept the Suitors off for ten years, not merely by the stratagem of the web but by other postpone- ments and evasions. Despite long hours of tearful lamenta- tion for her lost husband she keeps her courage, and her sudden appearances among the Suitors reduce them to mo- mentary acquiescence, which cannot all be ascribed to good manners. Her prudence makes her suspicious, and that is why she is so slow to recognize Odysseus as her husband. She and Telemachus are supported by the swineherd Eu- maeus and the old nurse Euryclea, and though the first claim of these is their unswerving loyalty to their master, they display an innate nobility in their response to the de- mands made of them. The party of Odysseus on Ithaca is ho- mogeneous in that it is held together by loyalty to him and hatred of the Suitors. It contains no very powerful personal- ity except the great man himself, but its members are suffi- ciently distinctive to set him in a full perspective. . . .

HOMER'S SETTING SUN

In general the *Odyssey* lacks the sustained splendour of the *Iliad,* has fewer overwhelming moments and a less de- manding conception of human worth. The slaughter of the Suitors provides a thrilling climax but lacks the profound pathos of the death of Hector, while the cold, vengeful anger of Odysseus is not comparable to the fiery, devouring pas- sion of Achilles. All is set in a lower key, and this may be due to the nature of the subject and the traditional treatment of it. Folktales and fairy-tales, even tales of injured wives and revengeful husbands, need not summon the same powers as the wounded pride of Achilles or the fate of Troy. The *Odyssey* has moments of breathless excitement and moving pathos, but its normal level is less stirring and closer to or- dinary experience. Even if tradition was partly responsible for setting this tone, there may be an additional reason for it in the poet's desire to compose a poem nearer to the life that he knew and to the events of every day. By combining these with impossible adventures and enthralling marvels he could set them in a new and brighter light. [The third- century A.D. Roman philosopher Cassius] Longinus thinks that this difference between the *Iliad* and the *Odyssey* is due to the poet's advancing years, and he makes a good observa- tion when he says:

Accordingly, in the *Odyssey* Homer may be compared to the setting sun, whose greatness remains without its intensity. He does not here maintain so high a level as in those poems of Ilium. His sublimities are not even sustained and free from sinking; there is not the same profusion of passions one after another, nor the supple and public style, packed with inventions drawn from real life. *(On the Sublime* 9.13)

Homer's Accurate Depiction of Seafaring in the *Odyssey*

Ernle Bradford

Because the *Odyssey* depicts many years of sailors'
wanderings through both charted and uncharted
seas, the work contains numerous references to and
descriptions of ships, oars, sails, prevailing winds,
beachings, and other aspects of ancient seafaring.
This essay by Ernle Bradford, a classical scholar
noted for his fine biography of Cleopatra, is an
excerpt from his book *Ulysses Found*, a fascinating
study of the Mediterranean islands and sailing routes
that may have, through sailors' tales, given rise to
many of the stories Homer told in the *Odyssey* (note
that Bradford uses the Roman name for Odysseus—
Ulysses). Comparing modern Greek and Italian
sailing vessels, geographical locations, and known
prevailing winds with those described in the *Odyssey*,
Bradford shows that much of Homer's portrayal of
ancient sailors, ships, and seafaring was accurate.

The island of Tenedos lies a bare two miles off the coastline
of Asia Minor. Between the island and the shore the fast-
running current still sluices down from the Dardanelles, just
as it did when the Greeks set sail from Troy. Now known as
Bozcaada, it is one of the only two Turkish islands in the
Aegean and is of little importance today. Indeed, its whole
history has been a happy one—happy in that it has hardly
featured in the bloody chronicles of the Aegean, except on
the one famous occasion when the Greeks pretended to
abandon the siege of Troy. When, on the instructions of
Ulysses, the Greeks had burned their camp and retreated to
their boats as if in defeat, it was towards Tenedos that they
set sail. It was nightfall when they left, and on the following

morning the Trojans coming out from their city found the Greek camp burned and deserted, and only the mysterious wooden horse left behind on the shore in front of Troy. The Trojans looked seaward, but there was no sign of the enemy fleet, so they assumed that the Greek ships were already hull-down, bound for their homeland. Little did they know, as they dragged the horse across the sun-dried land and into the walls of Troy, that the Greek fleet was lying concealed behind the low bulk of Tenedos. . . .

On the night when Ulysses and the other Greeks emerged from the belly of the wooden horse to open the gates of Troy, Agamemnon and the fleet rowed silently back from their shelter behind Tenedos. They beached their ships, and made their final victorious assault on the sleeping city of their enemies. It is likely that the Greeks anchored their fleet in the small bay just south of Yukyeri Point. It is still a good anchorage for small vessels, with a bottom of sand and weed, and a beach protected from the north by a small headland on which now stand the ruins of an old fort. Even though the coastline may have changed a little during the past three thousand years, it was probably here that the Greek fleet was drawn up during the siege of Troy. The low peninsula still provides shelter from the prevailing winds and the current runs more slowly at this point. Out in the centre, between Tenedos and the mainland, it can run as fast as two-and-a-half knots, a considerable hazard for ships which under sail or oar are unlikely to have made more than four or five.

It was from this beach that Ulysses embarked with his comrades after the sack of Priam's capital. Behind them the city on the plain still smoked, and the ruined walls collapsed with a sighing fall. A south-easterly wind was blowing, hot off the mainland, as they hauled in the sleeping-stones which served them for anchors and cast off the stern hawsers that they had made fast to rocks on the beach.

SHIPS WITHOUT NAMES

For ten years Ulysses was now condemned to wander the scrolled waters of the Mediterranean, knowing dawn and sunset always to the same background of sea-smell, and pitch-pine, and wet wood. Even the places where he was detained during his travels were no more than small anchorages, humped shoulders of rock, scrub and trees, from which the sea was always visible. His ship, which in those years he grew to know better than other men know their houses, was similar in some respects to the Viking craft which in later centuries were to cross the North Sea and the Atlantic—and even make their way into those warm stretches of the Mediterranean around Sicily, where Ulysses was now destined to sail.

PRECAUTIONS TAKEN BY ANCIENT SKIPPERS

In this excerpt from his famous book, The Ancient Mariners, *scholar Lionel Casson describes some of the dangers early Mediterranean sailors faced and how they tried to avoid them.*

Whether under sail or oars, working these ships was strenuous, uncomfortable, and dangerous. They were much less sturdy than the robust craft of the Vikings, and the Greeks were correspondingly far less bold than those reckless sea raiders. When Nestor, for example, sailed home from Troy, his first leg was fifteen miles to the island of Tenedos, his second an all-day run of fifty to Lesbos. Here he held a full-scale conference of his captains to plot the next course. With great trepidation he elected to strike out straight across the open sea instead of island hopping, made it safely to the southern tip of Euboea—and, on landing, set up a great sacrifice to Zeus, "thanking him for crossing that vast stretch of sea," all of one hundred and ten miles. Usually skippers stuck to the shore, sailing from one landfall to the next. When they had to travel at night they steered by the stars, but they avoided such voyages as much as possible. They much preferred to put in at evening, running the vessel smartly up a beach or, if there was none handy, throwing over the stone anchor in some shallow protected cove; this gave an opportunity to refill the water jars as well as to provide a night's sleep for all hands. On top of all these precautions, they limited their sailing to the time of year when the weather was most dependable, putting their boats in the water at the beginning of spring, around April, and hauling them out in October or so, when the fall set in. Practically all maritime activity, whether peaceful or warlike, was squeezed into the period between these months, and this remained more or less the case throughout the whole of ancient times.

. . . The ship of Ulysses has no recorded name. Some authorities . . . have seen in this evidence that the writer of the *Odyssey* had little knowledge of, or interest in, the sea and seafarers. Nothing could be further from the truth, for the

anthropomorphic habit of giving ships names is comparatively modern, although it is true we have record of ships'
names in classical times. I have sailed out of Trapani and the
Aegadian islands west of Sicily in recent years, in boats similar to those which the Homeric heroes used, and found on
them only the official registration numbers which they were
compelled to carry by the Italian Government. . . . Like the
Homeric vessels they are open boats, shallow-drafted and
keel-less, designed for being run up on beaches. Yet these
20th-century fishermen still go a hundred miles or more to
fish the rich banks off the North African coast. They have a
central rudder—something that Ulysses did not have—and
sometimes, but not always, a compass.

The number of men to each boat in Ulysses' squadron
probably varied, but it seems unlikely that many of them
were powered by more than twenty oars, ten to each side.
This would necessitate a minimum crew of twenty, but since
for long periods in the Mediterranean a vessel must be con-
stancy under oars, each one almost certainly carried at least
a double complement. The rowers could thus take watches.
But, quite apart from ensuring a change of men, such a system would have been necessary to make certain chat there
were always fresh men available to provide landing parties
when it came to the piracy that was an integral part of the
Homeric chieftain's life. Presuming that Ulysses left Troy
with twelve ships, the same number which he had brought
with him from the islands, it seems reasonable to assess the
total number of his force at about five hundred men. There
could have been more, for some of the ships might have
been bigger than others, but on this matter Homer is silent.

'SWIFT,' 'HOLLOW,' AND 'BLACK'

Greece was well-forested in those days and particularly rich
in pine. Pine has always been a good wood for the planking
and masting of ships, although oak is preferable for keels
and frames, and may well have been used. Common epithets
which are applied to ships in the Homeric poems are 'swift',
'well-balanced', 'hollow', and 'black'. 'Swift' in these terms is
clearly used to distinguish a war-galley from the more
beamy trading vessel. "Well-balanced' is still a nautical term
for any vessel that handles well, particularly when it is applied to a sailing vessel. 'Hollow' will surely mean an open
boat, or one that is not decked-in. This was basically true of

the Homeric ship, except that it would seem to have had a partially-enclosed section at the bows and stern. The forepart was no doubt used as a storage space, and the afterpart was where the master, the helmsman, and other people of note had their quarters. There was no truly enclosed cabin, such as one finds even in a small modern yacht. The Homeric ship was designed for short passages. Whenever possible, it was beached at night while the crew went ashore, made their fire for a meal, and slept out in the open, in a near-by cave, or sometimes under the mainsail which could be spread over a tent-like arrangement of oars.

Odysseus Builds a Boat

This passage from E.V. Rieu's translation of the Odyssey, *in which Odysseus fashions the craft he will use to leave Calypso's island, is the earliest description of shipbuilding in literature.*

Twenty trees in all he felled, and lopped their branches with his axe; then trimmed them in a workmanlike manner and trued them to the line. Presently Calypso brought him augers. With these he drilled through all his planks, cut them to fit across each other, and fixed this flooring together by means of dowels driven through the interlocking joints, giving the same width to his boat as a skilled shipwright would choose in designing the hull for a broad-bottomed trading vessel. He next put up the decking, which he fitted to ribs at short intervals, finishing off with long gunwales down the sides. He made a mast to go in the boat, with a yard-arm fitted to it; and a steering-oar too, to keep her on her course. And from stem to stern he fenced her sides with plaited osier twigs and a plentiful backing of brushwood, as some protection against the heavy seas. Meanwhile the goddess Calypso had brought him cloth with which to make the sail. This he manufactured too; and then lashed the braces, halyards, and sheets in their places on board. Finally he dragged her down on rollers into the tranquil sea.

The adjective 'black', so often applied to the ships, must certainly mean that they were tarred as a protection against wind and weather. The warm waters of the Mediterranean, then as now, were a favourable home for worm—the sinister, wood-loving *teredo* among others. Now tar has been used as a preventive against worm since the earliest days of navigation, and Ulysses was fortunate that one of the islands which came under his sway had its own natural pitch lake. 'Well-wooded Zacynthos' as it was always called, the modern Zante, lies about twenty miles south of Ithaca. Its pitch lake was first recorded by Herodotus in the 5th century B.C., but it is reasonable to assume that it had been in use since man first discovered the efficacy of pitch as a wood preservative. . . .

The Greek ships had been many years away from their home ports by the time that the siege of Troy was over, and one can only conclude that they brought with them large quantities of dried pitch for recaulking and anti-fouling. Under the hot sun of the northern Aegean, and in the luke-warm waters of midsummer, not a ship would have survived if they had not been carefully maintained by carpenters, shipwrights, caulkers and riggers. No doubt they made fires on the beaches and, once a year, melted down great slabs of pitch for repainting and preserving their vessels. (I have found worm in my own pine-planked sailing boat after only twelve months in the Mediterranean.)

Ulysses' ship is also sometimes described as 'blue'. No doubt her topsides above water were painted indigo, one of the earliest natural colours used by Mediterranean peoples. It is more than likely that she also had the 'oculus' or 'eye' painted on either bow. This custom which survives in the Mediterranean to this day derives from the ancient Egyptian Eye of Ra, the Sun-God, which was painted on their vessels many centuries before the Homeric period.

HOMERIC OARED GALLEYS

Such was Ulysses' home then, a swift, well-balanced, hollow, tarred boat, with probably ten oars a side. She carried one mast, almost certainly a fir spar, from which she set one square sail. The sail itself may have been of linen or papyrus, both of which materials the Egyptians had been exporting for centuries. There is a reference to a rope of papyrus in the house of Ulysses, but whether his sail was papyrus or linen, it is almost certain that his cordage will have been of papyrus and in some cases of leather. The sail was only set in moderate winds, and not expected to stand up to the strains which seamen would later demand from canvas.

The mast was movable, as is the case in many Mediterranean sailing boats to this date. It was housed in a sort of three-sided tabernacle and could be manhandled down so as to rest in a cradle in the stern. Supported by stays fore and aft, the mast will not have been very tall, since it needed only to support a square sail on a simple wooden yard. Quite large fishing and trading boats in the Gulf of Genoa and elsewhere use a similar type of mast and rigging to this day. When in harbour, the mast is invariably lowered to reduce top-weight and thus make the motion of the boat more comfortable for the men on board. I have no doubt that Ulysses and his men, when at anchor, often took their siestas—as I have done myself—under the shadow of the sail stretched across the lowered mast.

The oars, like the mast, will have been of fir and would seem to have been very broad in the blade—at least if the Homeric comparison of them to 'winnowing-shovels' may be taken at its face value. Quite apart from anything else, this would certainly account for the difficulty they often seem to have experienced in rowing against the wind. There were no rowlocks in the modem sense of the word. The oars were worked either over the gunwale, or through small ports in the ship's side against thongs of leather. Most Mediterranean boatmen, from the Aegean to the Tyrrhenian Sea, still prefer wooden thole-pins and a leather or rope grommet to metal rowlocks. . . .

The oared galley, which was the type of ship directly descended from those of the Homeric period, survived in the Mediterranean right into the 18th, and even the early 19th, century. The oared sailing vessel did not, in fact, disappear until very recent years when the advent of the mass-produced diesel engine gave the Mediterranean fishermen an alternative to oars during the long calms of mid-summer. For centuries after the English and the Scandinavian races had discarded oared vessels they were still in active use in the Mediterranean. The last naval action in which the oared galley predominated was the battle of Lepanto in 1571. . . . The galleys of Ulysses were a great deal smaller than [these]. . . . Under sail, and running free with the wind from abaft the beam, they may sometimes have made six knots or more. In view of Ulysses' later adventures with wind and weather, whirlpools and tidal streams, it is important to bear in mind how slow and small was the craft that he was sailing. Things which are simple and of little or no moment to a modern ship would have been terrifying and dangerous hazards to a sailor of the Homeric period. Quite apart from the size and comparative inefficiency of his craft, the early mariner was without chart or compass. He was venturing in a world where all was strangeness and mystery. It can hardly come as a surprise if his voyage came to be emblazoned with myth and fantasy by bards and storytellers.

FREE MEN, NOT SLAVES

If I have compared Ulysses' ship to a small galley, the men who pulled the oars were far from being galley-slaves. They were freeborn Greeks from the islands, and there was no conception at that time of the oar bench being a fitting place only for a slave. Ulysses refers to them as his 'friends', his 'companions', and his 'comrades', and there is never any suggestion that they were even of a lower caste than the hero himself. Centuries later, the Greeks who manned the galleys and defeated the Persian fleet at Salamis were all free men. It would seem that the galley-slave was a much later conception. . . . But, as anyone who has ever pulled an oar under the hot Mediterranean sun knows well, the degree of physical fitness and endurance required for long periods at the oar is immense. Whether one is a slave or not, the hardness of the life remains much the same. Jean Marteille de Bergerac, who was a French galley-slave in the 17th century, left some vivid descriptions of the life. 'Picture to yourself six men chained to a bench naked as they were born, one foot on the stretcher, the other lifted and placed against the bench in front of him, supporting in their hands a vastly heavy oar and stretching their bodies backwards while their arms are extended to push the loom of the oar clear of the backs of those in front of them. . . . Sometimes the galley-slaves row ten, twelve, even twenty hours at a stretch, without the slightest rest or break.' Now Ulysses' companions were not slaves, and the oars they handled were much smaller than those which de Bergerac was describing, yet there is no doubt that there were occasions when they had to row for many hours without a break. . . .

AN ILL-FATED VOYAGE

In a more or less open boat, with no charts or navigational instruments, and largely dependent upon the strength of the oarsmen, it was natural that the Homeric sailors should stick close to the shore whenever possible. At the first sign of approaching bad weather it was their custom to look for a suitable shelving beach, run the boat ashore, and wait until the danger was past and the sea had subsided.

When Ulysses and his ships left Troy it is more than likely that they made straight for Tenedos across the narrow strait. They would certainly not have ventured directly into the open sea south of the island, and it is probable that they made first for the anchorage at the north-eastern tip of Tenedos, where the fishing village of Bozcaada now stands. There was certainly a south-easterly blowing when they set sail, for in Book XI of the *Odyssey* Ulysses tells how 'the same wind that drove me from Troy brought me to Ismarus, the city of the Cicones.' Now the Cicones lived on the southern shores of Thrace, on that part of the mainland which faces across the sea towards the island of Samothrace. Their land lies north-west of Troy, so a square-sailed ship would need a south-easterly wind to be 'driven' to their shore. Something one cannot know is whether Ulysses had always intended to sail north and raid the Cicones. Perhaps in his opportunist's way he decided that the wind should not be wasted and that, while he and his men were in the northern Aegean, they might just as well do a little more looting before sailing home. . . .

Unfortunately, what should have been no more than a profitable diversion on the way home turned to disaster. The seal of ill-luck was set upon Ulysses' voyage from the very beginning.

Crime and Punishment in the *Odyssey*

George Dimock

The concept of retribution or penalty for serious wrongdoing constitutes one of the central themes of Homer's *Odyssey*. The most obvious example is the way the hero, Odysseus, must undergo years of wandering, loss, and suffering to satisfy the anger of some gods, particularly Poseidon, who feel they have been slighted. In this essay, George Dimock, a teacher of the classics at Smith College, explores other examples of crime followed by punishment in the *Odyssey*, including the episode in which Odysseus's men eat the sun god's cattle, the encounter with the uncivilized Cyclops Polyphemus, and the climactic confrontation with the suitors. Dimock makes the relevant point that there are also instances in the poem in which evil goes unpunished, suggesting that Homer was not so naïve as to believe that good will *always* triumph over bad.

Punishment for most of us is a word loaded with emotion. For a long time people in our culture have been intensely aware of many all-pervasive authorities: God, the church, the law, the government, society, our parents, all of which seem only too easy to anger and whose hostile reactions, that is, punishments, seem only too effective and painful. Greek literature on the whole is comparatively free from this degree of nervousness about authority, and that is one of its major attractions. Still, very early in its history there appears something very close to, in fact I would say identical with, what we mean by "punishment," and the place it appears is in Homer's *Odyssey*. As might be expected, what Homer has to say about it is not without interest.

If one were to ask, "What is the *Odyssey* about essen-

Excerpted from "Crime and Punishment in the *Odyssey*" by George Dimock, *Yale Review*, vol. 60, no. 2, December 1970, pp. 199–208. Reprinted by permission of Blackwell Publishers.

tially?" one would have to reply, I think, that it is about evil, evil in the sense of all those things about life which we don't like: toil, suffering, danger, the hostility of man and nature. Odysseus is introduced at once as the Great Sufferer:

> The man sing, Muse, devious, full of resources,
> driven all over the world when he sacked sacred Troy.
> Many men's cities he saw, and knew what man's mind is;
> many too were the evils his heart endured on the waters,
> keeping his ghost from Hades and bringing his men safe
>   homeward.
> Yet his men he could not save, hard though he tried to
>   protect them:
> their own weakness of mind brought them their undoing.
> Fools! They ate the cattle of Helios, god of the Sun—
> ate; and the god took from them the day of their
>   homecoming.

This introduction suggests both evil and human responsibility for it. We may reflect that Odysseus would not have suffered at least these particular evils if he had not made the long and dangerous journey to sack sacred Troy; his men, for their part, certainly would have done better not to eat Helios' cows. They unquestionably, and possibly Odysseus as well, were punished, and that is our topic.

THEIR PUNISHMENT SEEMS RIGHT

The eating of the Sun's cattle, in fact, when we come to it in the course of the poem, turns out to afford a remarkably complete example of what I think we mean by punishment. Not only is there the angered authority and the hostile reaction, but there is the suggestion that the authority is right and just, and that the offending action could and should have been avoided. The Sun, as Homer tells the story, seems a beneficent being who would be quite right to carry out his threat to shine among the dead if Odysseus' men were allowed to get away with their disrespect for him, for their crime is portrayed as a choice of death over life. Their ringleader Eurylochus says that even if Helios and the other gods really are going to sink them, he would prefer to end it all with one gulp of sea water than to spin out the pain on the desert island where they find themselves. So they eat Helios' cattle. They turn their backs on life, and if people are going to do that, we feel, the Sun might as well go and shine among the dead. Their punishment seems right. Furthermore, as I have said, it could have been avoided. Eurylochus and his friends were told what would happen, and at first resisted the temptation to eat the cattle. It was only as a result of their second and worser thoughts induced by hunger that they decided that perhaps, after all, they might get away with it. . . .

For similar reasons, Odysseus' slaughter of the suitors is not a murder, though it is sometimes called one. The suitors, wilfully blind, put their own heads in the noose. Very likely their wooing of Penelope was legitimate in the beginning, but from the first moment that we see them they are already in the wrong. They have taken over an absent man's house in despite of his wife and son. To be sure, they partly regard this as a way of putting pressure on Penelope to marry, and in the assembly they try to give it some color of legitimacy; but it is not legitimate. Their only answer to Mentor's charge of violence is the threat of force: "Even though you outnumber us," says Leiocritus in effect, "do you really want to fight about a dinner? We can play the 'superior numbers' game too. If Odysseus himself should come and try to chase us out, we would kill him." The assembly allows itself to be cowed, and it does seem as though the suitors might get away with it. Besides, it is so pleasant and convenient for them to spend the days feasting in Odysseus' house while they wait for Penelope to make up her mind. When she does, their announced plan, at least if Telemachus can somehow be got rid of, is to let her and her chosen husband keep the house while they divide the rest of the property. Obviously this is not a legitimate sequel to a legitimate wooing and wedding. . . . The suitors know they are wrong. . . . They refuse to believe that the gods are on the side of right against might, and as a result they enact for us that spectacle with which we are only too familiar, of unprincipled power behaving with what seems to be impunity. They should of course have known better, and it should be no surprise when punishment catches them after all. . . .

EVIL IS NOT ALWAYS PUNISHED

The *Odyssey* then, I think, is saying something important about a phenomenon which we may legitimately call crime and punishment. Homer's poem suggests that there is an order in events which assists what we instinctively feel to be the right and punishes what we feel to be wrong, regardless of the apparent distribution of power. Like Odysseus, we feel that individual men, high or low, strong or weak, are to be respected. Telemachus' very helplessness in the presence of one-hundred-eight hairy-chested suitors wins our sympathy and heightens our sense of outrage. We are glad when the gods' decree, his own enterprise, and his father's strength and cunning vindicate him.

Two questions remain: first, satisfactory as all this is, isn't it rather naïve of Homer to suggest that the good are rewarded and the bad punished in what we are accustomed to regard as a wicked and rather more complicated world; and second, what about the suggestion that Odysseus too may be being punished?

As for the first question, as soon as we begin to think about it, we see that Homer is not naïve. For one thing, evil is not always punished in the *Odyssey.* The Laestrygonians are at least as savage and, as Homer makes clear, as loathsome in their behavior as the Cyclops is. They too eat his men. But they are not punished; instead they destroy Odysseus' fleet, all but his own ship. Similarly there is nothing he can do about Scylla if he wishes to escape Charybdis. Odysseus, like the rest of us, has to face up to the experience of evils which are simply too strong for him. Evil is not always punished.

Secondly, when justice does triumph, Homer makes it seem reasonable and natural that it should. . . . Take the case of the Cyclops, who is brought low by the disadvantages inherent in his own savage lawlessness. In the first place, recognizing no need for restraint, he drinks too much. Secondly, without law or any restraining norms of social behavior, the Cyclopes are unable to live together or to develop any of the techniques of civilization, especially those which involve cooperation. As Homer says, they neither sow nor reap. They cannot travel about in the world for they do not know how to make boats. Nor, so long as they behave as they do, is their life likely to be enriched by the visits of others, a point explicitly made to Polyphemus by Odysseus. No wonder then that Polyphemus has neither the experience nor the imagination to conceive how a tiny weakling like Odysseus can harm him. He does not know the power of brains and technique even though he has a certain low cunning of his own. The result is that the weakling Odysseus by securing the cooperation of other weaklings like himself succeeds in boring out the Cyclops' eye, using a technique which, as Homer explicitly says, is part of the civilized art of ship-building. Odysseus' triumph then is not arbitrary. Uncivilized savagery, however great its brute strength, is at an obvious disadvantage against civilization through its very lawlessness, and Homer tells the story in such a way as to make us specifically aware of this.

RIGHT IS MORE APPEALING THAN WRONG

The suitors, by contrast, are civilized; yet they too, in spite of their superiority in numbers, suffer from inherent disadvantages. Fittingly, one of these is the opposite one to the Cyclops'. They are too civilized. Though they have set themselves against the laws and customs of their human society, they cannot do it thoroughly enough to succeed, for they are too squeamish. In particular, they do not kill Telemachus when they have the chance. As we have seen, the minute the suitors' ambush failed it was clear to Antinous that they would either have to kill Telemachus at once, or give up their fatal wooing. . . .

[But] the suitors neither accept the logic of the course they have embarked on and kill Telemachus, nor do they give up that course. They do not even consult the gods, but instead continue on their fatal way. Though they are at least partly and part of the time conscious that they have undertaken to oppose the laws of gods and men, children of civilization that they are they cannot make their opposition thorough enough to succeed. . . .

Another point which Homer makes in the case of the suitors is that right is just plain more appealing than wrong; it is, after all, the way people think things ought to be and be done. In view of this fact the suitors should not be as surprised as they are at Telemachus' success in bringing off his trip to Pylos and Sparta. In the assembly in the second book they are confident that even with Mentor and Halitherses on his side he will be unable to win enough support to put a ship in the water, but they are grievously mistaken. Their anxious questions once they discover he has gone accentuate this:

> Tell me the truth; when did he go and who were the
>   followers
> he had with him? The pick of the town, or was it his own
> hired help and house slaves? He could have done that.
> Tell me this truly also; I want to know clearly:
> by force, you not willing, he took your black ship,
> or willingly was it you gave what he asked for?

Only now do they discover their error. Noëmon answers:

> I myself willingly gave it. What would anyone else do,
> supposing a man like that, with all those cares on his soul,
> should ask it? To refuse a favor like that would be hard.

Because Telemachus is a victim of violence and injustice, people like Noëmon are more ready to help him. Right, especially in the underdog, is more appealing than wrong. It is not long before the suitors themselves are afraid that it will win out altogether.... Evidently Telemachus, even without Odysseus, has managed to make one-hundred-eight suitors afraid of him, and Homer makes this seem reasonable. Apparently right has considerable advantages on its side.

HOMER'S MORALITY

Yet when all is said and done Homer does suggest that the gods interfere on the side of right; that the good man is, in our terms, luckier than the bad one. Odysseus in the Cyclops' cave is conscious of divine help: perhaps Polyphemus suspected something, he says, and so brought the rams inside the cave the night he was blinded, or perhaps the gods impelled him to. In any case, it was lucky, for the rams provided the means of escape. And again, Odysseus feels it was very lucky that his men's nerve did not fail at the crucial moment of boring out the Cyclops' eye. He does everything he can to keep their spirits up himself, but even so when the moment comes, he gives the credit to the gods. Similarly in the slaying of the suitors, Athene's help, though slight, is crucial. Here we must admit a fundamental difference between Homer's picture of the world and our own, for we cannot accept, as he does, the idea of divine interference with the natural course of events. Yet at a still more fundamental level I think we will find ourselves in agreement with him. What made the difference between punishment and mere revenge, we recall, was the feeling that the final authority was the gods, or Zeus. Odysseus' sense that he had not done it all himself was what kept him from vaunting above the slain. Conversely, the blind wilfulness of those who commit crime in the *Odyssey* consists ultimately in their failure to recognize anything superior to their own will. They do think they "do it all themselves." "We are much stronger than the gods," says the Cyclops in his ignorance; and, "Don't ever, yielding to foolishness, talk so big again," says Odysseus' cowherd to the suitor he has just killed; "let the gods have the say-so, for they are much stronger." The point is that whether or not heaven "really" intervenes in particular cases, right is stronger than anybody. Homer has not, after all, given us a false picture of the world.

Herein lies the refutation of the charge sometimes made that the morality of the *Odyssey* is the morality of the concentration camp, that Odysseus' right to his possessions, his family, and his kingdom, and above all his right to punish the suitors, is simply the right of the stronger, of superior military effectiveness. What keeps this from being true is Odysseus' own recognition that there is something in the world bigger, more powerful, and more important than he is, something which makes the rules and in one way or another enforces them. Cyclopes, suitors, and Nazis, on the other hand, all operate on the assumption that their own will, individual or collective, is supreme; that there is no reason to refrain from doing anything they wish which seems within their powers; that accordingly the weak and hungry, guests, suppliants, and beggars never need to be respected. On this point, there is no question that the poem sides with Odysseus and against the concentration camp. Homer's morality, I think we must conclude, is ultimately neither repugnant nor naïve.

Why Does Wise Penelope Act So Rashly?

Frederick M. Combellack

In most of the scenes in which Penelope appears in
the *Odyssey*, Homer presents her as a wise woman,
in many ways the intellectual equal of her husband,
the shrewd Odysseus. Yet, as Frederick M. Combellack, professor emeritus of classics at the University
of Oregon, points out, in the passages in which she
interacts with the disguised Odysseus, thinking him
to be a beggar, she shows signs of having made a
rash and seemingly needless decision. She has made
up her mind that she may as well go ahead and
marry one of the suitors, despite having recently
learned that her long-lost husband might at that very
moment be back in Ithaca. Attempting to explain this
apparent discrepancy in the text, Combellack offers
the views of some leading Homeric scholars, as well
as his own.

Homer defines Penelope for us in a series of repeatedly emphasized pairs: her main qualities are her beauty and her
prudence. Her deepest prevailing emotions are longing for
her husband's return and loathing for the thought of a second marriage. Her main activities are weeping and sleeping.
Of course, she weaves, like all of Homer's women, but nothing much is made of this. She has no scene corresponding to
the picture of Helen coming into her great hall with her
maids, her silver work basket, and her blue wool. We are not
even told anything about the pattern in her cloth, as we are
told in the *Iliad* that Helen's weaving showed the battles of
the Greeks and the Trojans. This is the more remarkable in
that her weaving of Laertes' shroud is an important element
in the background of Homer's story. But even this is kept in
the background, and it is not until the very last book of the

Reprinted from Frederick M. Combellack, "Wise Penelope and the Contest of the Bow,"
California Studies in Classical Antiquity, vol. 6, pp. 32–46. Copyright ©1974 by the
Regents of the University of California. Reprinted by permission of the University of
California Press.

poem that we are told that this piece of cloth was large and shone like the sun or the moon.

ODYSSEUS IN BEGGARLY GUISE

Our problem concerns the character of Penelope, her situation, and one of her actions, as these are portrayed in the *Odyssey*. If the relevant evidence is to be clearly before us, we must examine in some detail some parts of the poem. In Book 19, after Odysseus and Telemachus have removed the arms from the hall, Penelope, looking like Artemis or golden Aphrodite, leaves her room, comes into the hall, and sits by the fire on a chair decorated with ivory and silver, a chair made by the craftsman Icmalius. The scene has been impressively set for the long-postponed first conversation between Penelope and Odysseus, an Odysseus still in the beggarly guise imposed upon him by Athena. The rest of the book is given over to this scene.

The beggar makes a fine impression on Penelope, convincing her that he entertained Odysseus for a fortnight in Crete twenty years earlier. Before, she had regarded him only with pity; now he will be a respected friend. Having won her confidence, the beggar then announces that he just recently heard that Odysseus is close to Ithaca. Indeed, he would have arrived some time ago had he not decided to go to Dodona [site of the famous religious oracle dedicated to Zeus] to ask whether he should return to his native land openly or in secret. The beggar swears an oath that Odysseus will very soon be home. . . . "I could well wish that this would happen," says Penelope, "but I think Odysseus will not come home now."

After the longish episode of the footbath (during which Penelope sits distracted by Athena), Penelope speaks again to the beggar, this time in more intimately personal terms. She describes her own miseries during these long lonely years and then turns to the presently pressing problem: should she continue as she has been, staying with her son and watching over the property, or should she marry the best of the suitors? While Telemachus was a child, he kept her from marrying again, but now the pressure from him works the other way; he is concerned about the property which the suitors are destroying.

She then asks the beggar to interpret her dream of the eagle who came and killed her flock of geese and then, as she wept over the dead geese, returned and told her that the geese were really the suitors and that he who was an eagle is now her husband Odysseus. The beggar sensibly replies that Odysseus has himself interpreted her dream for her in the only possible way. "Dreams are hard to interpret," says Penelope, "and those that come through the ivory gate are deceitful. Those that come through the horn gate are reliable, but I don't think my dream came from there."

It is at this point that Penelope announces that tomorrow she will leave Odysseus's home. She will set the contest of the bow and the axes, and the winner of the contest will take her away from the beautiful, wealthy home, "which I think I shall remember even in my dreams." Odysseus urges her to set the contest (and well he might); and Penelope, after a few gracious words to the beggar, goes up to her room and cries herself to sleep.

WEAVING THE SHROUD

This scene in Book 19 is enough in itself to make us ask why it is that Penelope, who has waited so long, and who regards a second marriage with such horror, makes up her mind to choose a second husband, when she has just been thinking about this remarkably clear dream (we are not told when she had the dream) and has just received from the apparently reliable beggar the assurance under oath that Odysseus will very soon be home.

There is reasonably clear evidence in the poem that Penelope has long been under considerable pressure to marry again and that this pressure has very recently been greatly increased. Once or twice in the poem we are told that her father and her brothers are eager for her to marry. Some three or four years ago, when Telemachus was about seventeen and might be felt to be at least approaching manhood, there had apparently been a vigorous effort to get her to marry. To avoid marriage, she had hit upon the device of Laertes' shroud, and it would seem that the agreement had been that if the suitors would wait until the weaving was finished then Penelope would, on completing the shroud, choose a second husband. For three years Penelope enjoyed a kind of precarious security, weaving by day, unraveling by night, until her trick was discovered because of the treachery of one of the servants. That the trick worked so long says more for the cleverness of Penelope than for the intelligence of the suitors. . . . We must conclude that Odysseus's arrival in Ithaca followed close upon the completion of the shroud. At the time of the opening of the *Odyssey*, Penelope has very recently finished the weaving, at most only a week or two ago, very possibly only a few days ago. I do not know whether the fact that the weaving has just been completed should make us feel that Penelope should be more willing or less willing to put off the hated decision for another week or so. I should expect that, if anything, a fortnight's delay might seem more reasonable under the very recently increased pressure than if she had already delayed for some time. . . .

THE PROBLEM WITH PRUDENT PENELOPE

Another factor which is relevant to our judgment on Penelope's conduct is the prophecy of Theoclymenus. Earlier on this very same day on which Penelope makes her decision, she had been told under oath by the prophet Theoclymenus that Odysseus was actually in Ithaca planning evil for the suitors. Penelope courteously replies, "I could certainly wish that what you say might be true. If so, you would receive such gifts from me that anyone who met you would say that you were a lucky man."

Finally, in her remarks to the suitors in Book 18, Penelope said that when Odysseus left for Troy he told her to marry again if he had not returned by the time Telemachus was bearded.

We may now summarize Penelope's situation at the moment when she announces to the beggar her decision to choose a new husband by means of the bow contest:

Very recently, maybe only a few days ago, she has finished the weaving which enabled her to put off the hated decision for some years. Her father and her brothers have made it clear that they think she should marry again, though we cannot be sure when their influence was first brought to bear. She is herself aware that postponing the marriage is unfair to Telemachus, since it involves a steady depletion of his inheritance. And Telemachus is now at an age when Odysseus told her to marry again, though it is not certain either when he first arrived at this age. These are the factors impelling Penelope to take the step she does, and it must be agreed that their cumulative weight is considerable. None of the factors, however, is of a sort to require her to make an *immediate* decision instead of delaying for, say, a week or two if, in addition to her deep-seated reluctance, there are any other factors which counsel a short further postponement. Homer has made the presence of such factors abundantly clear. A few hours ago a prophet has solemnly assured her that Odysseus is actually in Ithaca. This very night, while the beggar has been having his footbath, she has been musing on this dream whose transparent meaning is that the suitors will be killed by her husband. And the beggar, who has impressed her so favorably that he has now become a respected guest and friend, has just solemnly assured her that Odysseus is not far from Ithaca and will very soon be home. An important feature of the statements by the prophet and the beggar is that only a very short time will be necessary to test their truthfulness.

Our problem is distressingly clear: why does the prudent Penelope resolve to marry again at this precise moment when she has no overpowering reasons for an immediate decision and does have these plausible reasons for at least a short delay?

READING BETWEEN HOMER'S LINES

There have, of course, been various attempts to answer this question. One answer has recently been restated by [Homeric scholars Denys] Page and [G.S.] Kirk: Penelope's illogical decision, taken together with some other features of the poem . . . "supports the probability that an earlier version, in which the contest was arranged in full collusion between husband and wife, has been extensively but inadequately remodelled by the large-scale composer." Whether or not we are prepared to accept this theory, we must, I think, admit that it cannot be disproved. Unlike many guesses about what lies back of Homer, this guess is supported by an unusually large number of details in the poem which are otherwise at the least somewhat odd. The oddities have been well discussed by Page and Kirk, and there is no need to rehearse them here.

Among the Unitarians [those scholars who hold that Homer was the sole author] the closest approach to this explanation is probably that in Chapter X of W.J. Woodhouse's *The Composition of Homer's Odyssey.* In Woodhouse's view, Homer has reached an impasse in his plot. "Willy nilly, one or other of the actors in the story must do something, in

order that the whole thing may go forward. If the poet cannot find in his characters what he needs in the way of mo-
tive power, he must just contribute it out of his own head."
So here, the story must go on, even at the cost of consistency
in Penelope's character. For Woodhouse, as for Page and
Kirk, Homer's difficulties are rooted in his sources. But for
Woodhouse, these are various old "Tales," not a different
version of the *Odyssey.*

It was inevitable that solutions such as these should seem
to some of Homer's admirers an outrageous aspersion on
Homer's craftsmanship. An important element in the
derogatory explanation is that in some of Homer's sources,
whether earlier "Odysseys" or "Tales," husband and wife are
identified to each other before the slaughter of the suitors.
We have recently been asked to believe that in our *Odyssey*
Penelope really penetrates Odysseus's disguise before she
decides on the contest of the bow. This view has been presented in two able articles by P.W. Harsh and the late Anne
Amory. I am not sure I have read any suggestion about difficulties in Homer which I should accept with more pleasure
than this one, if I thought it were possible. There are, however, two reasons for rejecting it, either of which would be
fatal even alone. In the first place, the theory requires us to
assume that Homer, regularly the most straightforward and
lucid of poets, has chosen to wrap an important feature of
his story in a mystery which we can penetrate only by reading between his lines and assuming that he meant things
which he did not say. I should think nearly everyone would
agree that Homer is not that kind of poet.

The second objection to the theory is contained in
Homer's picture of Penelope at the beginning of the next
book. After her talk with the beggar, Penelope goes up to her
room and weeps for Odysseus until Athena puts her to sleep.
(Even this does not seem altogether appropriate for a
woman who believes that Odysseus is home.) Book 20 opens
with a picture of the sleepless Odysseus, who is finally also
put to sleep by Athena. But as he falls asleep, Penelope
wakes up. She cries and wails and calls upon Artemis to kill
her at once.... Better to go down under the earth than to
gladden the heart of an inferior man. All this fits perfectly
with the Penelope whom Homer has just described, resolved
to choose a second husband tomorrow, but hating the
thought of it. But Penelope's words are completely incom-

patible with the Harsh-Amory woman who knows that Odysseus is asleep downstairs. . . .

WHAT SHE SHOULD HAVE DONE

We have seen good reason to wonder at Penelope's conduct, but we are not yet through with her. The timing of her resolve to choose a new husband has been much discussed, and many have found her conduct here out of keeping with her character. But there is another aspect of her conduct which is even more inexplicable.

Homer has portrayed for us a woman whose intelligence is frequently emphasized in the poem, and in Book 23 he shows her more than a match for the brilliant Odysseus himself. He has also emphasized that she is under great pressure to marry again. Finally he has made it clear that the thought of a second marriage fills her with such loathing that even death seems preferable. How is such a woman to solve her problem?

Some years ago she hit upon the device of the shroud. She cannot have imagined that this would be more than a delaying action. Indeed, she must have been remarkably sanguine if she expected the delay to be as long as it actually was. This useful device has now lost its usefulness. What can she do next? The obvious answer, I should think, is look for another device. The really amazing thing about the intelligent Penelope's conduct is that it does not occur to her that she has ready to hand another device which will not merely postpone her second marriage, but will solve her problem permanently.

In the storeroom of her palace, there is a splendid bow, an heirloom from the great archers of an earlier generation. It is an extremely hard bow to string. With it Odysseus in the days before the war used to perform a difficult trick of shooting "through the axes" set up in his great hall. There is every reason to believe that no one but Odysseus (and possibly his son) could string the bow and shoot through the axes.

Penelope's problem almost solves itself. All she need do is pretend to the suitors that she has made up her mind to delay no longer. She has not, however, been able to decide which of her many suitors to choose, and so she will allow a contest with her husband's bow to make the decision for her. . . .

This, I suggest, is the obvious solution that should have occurred to the kind of woman Homer has portrayed. Her failure to think of it has long seemed to me the great defect in the plotting of the *Odyssey*. And Homer could have told the story in this way with only the slightest and easiest changes in the story as it now stands: one or two lines to tell us that Penelope's proposal is a trick and not seriously meant; one or two adding the proviso that will rid the house of the suitors; one or two telling us that after having decided on the pseudo-contest, she woke in the night and was reduced to despair as she wondered if one of the suitors might just possibly succeed. Everything else in the poem can be left exactly as it is. There is no need to tell the beggar that the contest is a trick; the suitors will fail to string the bow; Odysseus will get the bow into his hands, and the suitors will be destroyed. The story told in this form not only saves Penelope from any charge of illogical conduct, but also has a special appropriateness to the extremely intelligent woman we have been assured she is. In the story as we have it, Penelope, the model of cautious, shrewd intelligence, acts on this one occasion like a rash, precipitate fool. It is quite understandable that Homer's readers have often wondered why.

Deception Used for Comic Effect in the *Odyssey*

Reynold Z. Burrows

One of the hallmarks of Odysseus's character is his craftiness and gift for deceiving people. Perhaps the most familiar example of this gift occurs in the *Iliad*, when he conceives the plan for the Trojan horse, which is instrumental in the Greek victory. In keeping with the heroic but often grim tone of the *Iliad*, there is nothing humorous about this use of deception. The *Odyssey*, on the other hand, contends scholar Reynold Z. Burrows, formerly of Sweet Briar College, contains many examples of deception used for comic effect. He cites episodes involving Odysseus and other characters, including some of the gods, to support his argument that Homer's ancient audiences found the "dramatic interplay between deceiver and deceived" amusing and entertaining.

Human society, as depicted in the *Odyssey*, is genial and expansive; this is a world of unhurried moments, urbane, lighthearted, and courteous. The exigencies of *timê* or honor are still important, but less consciously so, in this fabled world where *all* is possible and where the goal of life is not glorious death on the battle-field as in the *Iliad*, but to explore and to survive with a passionate determination. Ingenuity replaces brawn, and in this world is far more important, since, indeed, the adversaries Odysseus meets are often superhuman, and he must use his wits to survive. Even in the case of the suitors their very number ranks the slaying with the marvelous, the unbelievable. Odysseus does survive by using his intellectual acuity, and, in particular, his ability to deceive, as for example in the episode of the Cyclops.

Excerpted from Reynold Z. Burrows, "Deception as a Comic Device in the *Odyssey*," *Classical World*, vol. 59, no. 2, October 1965, pp. 33–36. Reprinted by permission of *Classical World*.

DECEPTION A COMIC DEVICE?

When Odysseus lands in Ithaca and is asked by Athena in disguise who he is, the poet tells us that "it (the truth) was on the tip of his tongue, but ever loyal to his crafty nature he held it back.". . . This is the quality by which Homer wishes Odysseus to be identified; this tendency to deceive is not a "motiveless malignity" but an intellectual trademark, so to speak, without which Odysseus would lose his identity.

It was very aptly observed by [French moralist Jean de] LaBruyère in the Seventeenth Century that life is a comedy for the man who thinks and a tragedy for the man who feels. Odysseus is the thinking man *par excellence* in the literature of antiquity and he views his world of romantic adventure with a detachment and objectivity that rarely touches his innermost being, his deepest feelings. He meets vicissitudes with resignation and even with a degree of anticipation, however bitterly he may lament his belated return to Ithaca. But Odysseus seems *most* the thinking man when he is *most* the deceiving man, and consequently the deceptions in the Odyssey may be very closely linked with comedy. Furthermore, I believe that, at the same time, this element of deception, so necessary for survival, provides the *chief* source of comic amusement in the *Odyssey*. . . . We certainly know how frequently the device of mistaken identity is used on the comic stage. But in the *Odyssey* the element of deception affords the reader a very special and varied delight. In developing this point we should first inquire briefly and generally into the nature of the comic in Homer's *Odyssey*.

VARIOUS COMIC ELEMENTS

Clearly we must not attribute to Homer a comic intention where there probably was none. Telemachus in Book III of the *Odyssey* is asked politely, in all seriousness, and without any implication of moral opprobrium whether he is a pirate or not. Odysseus boasts to the Phaeacians that he is noble Odysseus and his fame reaches heavenward; there are many occasions when Odysseus moans and groans when beset by real or imaginary dangers, behaving according to the standards of Homer's society: these situations seem comic enough to us, given our cultural values, but it is open to doubt that they appeared so to Homer.

Undoubtedly, elements comic to both Homeric society and to our own do exist in the *Odyssey*, such as the farcical episodes involving the Cyclops, the Sirens, and Aeolus; the coarse humor of the love of Ares and Aphrodite. There is the high comedy of manners played especially in the scenes with Nestor, Helen and Menelaus, Alcinous and Arete.... Knowing so little about the age in which the epic was created we are not in a position to detect satire, political, social, or religious; but the very nature of satire is topical and suggests an immediate context; consequently it would very probably be out of place in a work of such scope, grandeur, and timelessness as the *Odyssey*. One may detect some glimmers of mock epic, perhaps, as in the scene in Ithaca between Odysseus and Athena in Book XIII, in which Athena seems to be a parody and a burlesque of herself: when reproached by Odysseus, she appears somewhat pedestrian and a little silly in her excuses.

A DEFT INTERPLAY OF INTELLECTS

But Homer apparently found as the most intriguing ingredient of humor the device of deception, which appears so often in the *Odyssey*; the very frequency with which it occurs would seem to establish it as the supremely amusing and diverting expression of the comic. What was the Greek attitude toward lying and deception? Indeed, we know the delight all audiences feel in watching deception practiced: one feels smug superiority in the possession of knowledge denied to others. Further, the Greeks of antiquity were particularly enthralled by a good story told with effective delivery; in historical times adherence to the truth was often a secondary consideration, as we may judge, for example, from extant speeches of the orators and statements throughout Greek literature showing the paramount importance the Greeks placed on the art of persuasion, *the power to charm*; and we may be sure that the injunctions against falsehoods voiced by the moralists from time to time, although certainly desirable in the instances of political or forensic oratory, were still few and managed to exert little influence. One has only to recall the notorious example of brilliant Alcibiades [the controversial fifth-century B.C. Athenian politician], who, although a proven traitor, succeeded in winning over the affections of his fellow citizens. Evidently his persuasive charm and attractiveness counted for more than the record of his scandalous career. Returning to literary and dramatic fictions ... judging from the frequency in drama of deception scenes the average Greek must have derived much whimsical stimulation from this source, and in this respect the Greeks were like precocious children, who sometimes are willing partners in a playful deception because of the delight afforded by the imaginary, the inventive, by a shared intimacy; and when a skillful poet adds dramatic effects, proper diction, careful structure, and an illusion of spontaneity to the deception, the nimble and deft interplay of intellects, we reach something like artistic perfection. A kind of emotional rapport between the spectator and the characters is thus produced, quite outside the sphere of conscious moral considerations, and predicated on the quite correct assumption that beneath the superficial and literal falsehood is found the substratum of universal and poetic truth; and we must not forget that the poet was regarded fundamentally as a teacher.

ODYSSEUS' DEEP-SEA YARNS

We may then apply what we have said about deception portrayed in the drama to deception as we find it in the epic and we may infer a similar delight on the part of the reader or listener. We see that the Homeric gods themselves regularly practice deception, as in Athena's assumption of the form of Mentor and Mentes in the *Odyssey*, and in Hera's beguiling of Zeus in the *Iliad*, sometimes heartlessly and with disastrous results, as in *Iliad* XXII in which Achilles slays Hector aided by Athena who deceives the Trojan in the guise of his brother Deiphobus. Although a powerful device, deception when used in the works of Homer and other poets for the exploitation or undoing of an innocent individual (I omit, of course, the Cyclops), can arouse only indignation. We need only observe how often in the *Odyssey* Aegisthus and Clytemnestra are excoriated for their vile deception of Agamemnon. This, to be sure, has no connection, quite obviously, with the use of guile to produce a *comic* effect. In Book XIII of the *Odyssey* Athena actually praises Odysseus for his attempt to deceive her! "We are both adept at chicanery," she purrs and then proceeds to aid her favorite in his deception and slaying of the suitors.

The deep-sea yarns are unmistakable evidence of Homer's decided preference for the use of deception as a comic technique. All these occur in the last twelve books of the *Odyssey* and are told by Odysseus to Athena: Eumaeus, the loyal swineherd; Antinous one of the suitors; Penelope, his wife; and Laertes, his father. In some of these he pretends to a Cretan background and these stories have been thought to contain material of pre-Homeric saga which had become embedded in the Homeric poems. Indeed Homer is so intrigued with the comic possibilities of the yarns that he seems reluctant to let go of the idea. These yarns have similar material; if they had all been absolutely the same we could dismiss this similarity as repetitions (perhaps for the convenience of the reciter) such as are found elsewhere in the Greek epic. We might even say that Homer was nodding. But Homer evidently wished to exhibit here in the tales of Odysseus a most

ATHENA PRAISES ODYSSEUS FOR DECEIVING HER

This is an excerpt from the cleverly written scene in which Athena deceives Odysseus while he vainly attempts to deceive her.

Athena now appeared upon the scene. She had disguised herself as a young shepherd, with all the delicate beauty that marks the sons of kings. A handsome cloak was folded back across her shoulders, her feet shone white between the sandal-straps, and she carried a javelin in her hand. She was a welcome sight to Odysseus, who came forward at once and accosted her eagerly 'Good-day to you, sir,' he said. 'Since you are the first person I have met in this place, I hope to find no enemy in you, but the saviour of my treasures here and of my very life. . . . But what I beg of you first is to tell me exactly where I am. What part of the world is this? What is the country called and who live here?'. . .

'Sir,' said the goddess of the gleaming eyes, 'you must be a simpleton or have travelled very far from your home to ask me what this country is. It has a name by no means so inglorious as that. In fact it is known to thousands. . . . My friend, the name of Ithaca has travelled even as far as Troy; and that, they say, is a good long way from Achaea [Greece].'

Odysseus' patient heart leapt up as the divine Pallas Athena told him this, and he revelled in the knowledge that he was on his native soil. He answered her readily enough, but not with the truth. It had been on the tip of his tongue, but loyal as ever to his own crafty nature he contrived to keep it back.

'Of course,' he said, 'I heard tell of Ithaca even over there across the seas in the spacious land of Crete. And now I have come there myself with all these goods of mine, leaving the complex and varied comic effect, an effect considered at once psychologically engrossing and aesthetically pleasing, involving, as it does, a dramatic interplay between deceiver and deceived; and here too was abundant scope for the colorful depiction of the crafty, imaginative, vivacious, and knavish. With the poet's sure touch are revealed in these five tales the agility and spontaneity of Odysseus' intellect, his sympathetic power, his puckish wit, each tale rather appropriate to the person addressed and to the situation in which it occurs. . . .

The tales all start plausibly with genealogies. Homer has Odysseus pose often in these tales as a Cretan, one of a peo-

other half of my fortune to my children. For I had to take to my heels. I had killed Idomeneus' son, the great runner Orsilochus, who was faster on his feet than any living man in the whole island of Crete. He tried to fleece me of all the spoil I had won at Troy, my wages for the long-drawn agonies of war and all the miseries that sea-travel means, merely because I refused to curry favour with his father by serving as his squire at Troy. . . . I hastily sought out a Phoenician ship, threw myself on the mercy of its honest crew, and with a liberal donation from my booty persuaded them to take me on board. . . . We beat about for a time, and in the night we made this island and rowed the ship helter-skelter into harbour. . . . We all tumbled out of the ship and lay down just as we were. I was so exhausted that I fell sound asleep. Meanwhile the crew fetched my goods out of the good ship and dumped them down on the sand where I lay. After which they embarked once more and set sail for their own fine city of Sidon, leaving me and my troubles behind.'

The bright-eyed goddess smiled at Odysseus' tale and caressed him with her hand. Her appearance altered, and now she looked like a woman, tall, beautiful, and accomplished. And when she replied to him she abandoned her reserve.

'What a cunning knave it would take,' she said, 'to beat you at your tricks! Even a god would be hard put to it.

'And so my stubborn friend, Odysseus the arch-deceiver, with his craving for intrigue, does not propose even in his own country to drop his sharp practice and the lying tales that he loves from the bottom of his heart. But no more of this: we are both adepts in chicane. For in the world of men you have no rival as a statesman and orator, while I am pre-eminent among the gods for invention and resource.'

ple famous as sea-roving adventurers. The stories he tells
deal with elements common to the experience of Odysseus:
intrigue, shipwreck, piracy, adventure, a mutinous crew, descriptions of himself and his own adventures, but, rather
oddly, there is *nothing* of the supernatural in these tales;
there occur no such hair-raising adventures as those with
the Cyclops. Aeolus, Circe, Scylla, Charybdis. This is possibly
because these latter experiences do not occur in the realm of
plausibility, and Odysseus is endeavoring to persuade his lis-
teners of happenings within their understanding.

THE JOY OF DECEIVING

What then of the *Apologue to Alcinous*, Books IX–XII, in
which Odysseus tells of his adventures with fabled monsters? Could he in his playful way have concocted these stories of the marvelous just for the Phaeacians, an unearthly
people close to the gods and dwelling on the borders of a
fantastic world, stories within, so to speak, the limits of *their*
own experience, Odysseus knowing as he does "the minds of
men"? Is he being "true to his nature" here as well in carrying on a deception of never-never-land people? Only Calypso, the nymph who received him and with whom he
stayed for eight years, is not included in the *Apologue*, and it
is tempting to follow this reasoning in reaching an understanding of the character of Odysseus and the importance of
deception as an element of Homeric humor....

In conclusion, the tendency to deceive, then, that we find
first so predominant in Homer is, in the *Odyssey*, consistently employed for an intellectually comic effect, and
Homer is at pains to delight us with deception whenever ar-
tistically practicable even in the last book, in which
Odysseus cannot forego the joy of deceiving his own father
Laertes; true, he does desist, but not before the comic trickery has come close to tragedy; and consequently the effect of
this particular deception is quite stunning.

Chronology

B.C.

CA. 3000–1100

Bronze Age of Greece, in which people used bronze tools and weapons.

CA. 1400–1200

Mycenaean civilization dominates the Aegean sphere and utilizes a syllabary writing script modern scholars call Linear B.

CA. 1250

Date proposed for the Trojan War by fifth-century B.C. Greek historian Herodotus, shown by modern scholars to be essentially correct.

CA. 1200–1100

Perhaps after a period of civil strife among Mycenaean kingdoms, the Dorians, a warlike and culturally backward Greek-speaking people, invade Greece, causing the final collapse of Mycenaean civilization.

CA. 1100–800

Dark age of poverty and illiteracy in Greece.

CA. 850–750

Most likely period in which Homer, traditionally accepted as the author of the epic poems the *Iliad* and the *Odyssey*, lived.

CA. 750–700

The Greeks become literate again, this time employing the Phoenician alphabet.

566

Oral recitations of the Homeric epics become part of Athens's sacred religious festival, the Panathenaea.

CA. 550–530

Athenian leader Pisistratus commissions a group of scholars to commit the Homeric epics to writing (or perhaps to edit already existing written texts).

CA. 509–508

World's first democracy established in Athens; in Italy, a group of Rome's richest landowners throw out their king and establish the Roman Republic.

CA. 470–430

Athens's so-called golden age, during which it creates a powerful Mediterranean empire, expands its democracy, and builds the Parthenon and other magnificent temples atop its Acropolis.

336–323

Greek conqueror Alexander the Great spreads Greek culture throughout the Near East, including Egypt, where he establishes the city of Alexandria.

CA. 280–150

Zenodotus and other Greek scholars working in Alexandria compare and edit existing and differing versions of the *Iliad* and the *Odyssey*, eventually creating a standardized "vulgate" version of the epics that survives, with minor changes, into modern times.

146

Having defeated the Greek kingdoms established by Alexander's successors, Rome imposes direct rule on Greece.

A.D.

476

The Roman Empire ceases to exist as a political entity; in the following centuries, as medieval European kingdoms grow from its wreckage, Homer's epics survive in handwritten copies.

1488

First printed text of Homer's works appears in Florence, Italy.

1870

In an effort to prove that Homer's Troy was a real place, German archaeologist Heinrich Schliemann begins digging at Hisarlik, a mound in northwestern Turkey, and discovers several ancient cities built one on top of another; he eventually concludes that Troy II is the legendary city of the *Iliad.*

1876

Schliemann begins excavations at Mycenae, in southeastern Greece, initiating an age of archaeological discoveries of Mycenaean civilization and reappraisals of Homer's epics.

1922

Homer is popularized for many who have never read his works in Irish author James Joyce's novel *Ulysses,* which utilizes the framework and themes of the *Odyssey.*

1932–1938

A University of Cincinnati expedition led by American archaeologist Carl Blegen undertakes a thorough excavation of Hisarlik; Blegen shows that Troy VIIa, rather than Troy II, was likely the Homeric city.

1951

Scholar Richmond Lattimore publishes his highly acclaimed translation of Homer's *Iliad.*

1952

English amateur linguist Michael Ventris deciphers Linear B, showing that it is an archaic form of Greek and therefore that the Mycenaeans, Homer's Achaean heroes, were early Greeks.

1955–1956

Homer receives further popularization in two major films: the Italian *Ulysses,* based on the *Odyssey,* and the American *Helen of Troy,* depicting events from the *Iliad* and other epics from the Trojan cycle.

FOR FURTHER RESEARCH

NOTEWORTHY TRANSLATIONS OF HOMER'S *ILIAD* AND *ODYSSEY* (IN ORDER OF PUBLICATION)

Iliad. Translated by W.H.D. Rouse. New York: New American Library, 1950.

Iliad. Translated by E.V. Rieu. Baltimore: Penguin Books, 1950.

Iliad. Translated by A.H. Chase and W.G. Perry Jr. Boston: Little, Brown, 1950.

Iliad. Translated by Richmond Lattimore. Chicago: University of Chicago Press, 1951.

Iliad. Translated by Robert Fitzgerald. New York: Anchor-Doubleday, 1974.

Iliad. Translated by Michael Reck. New York: HarperCollins, 1994.

Odyssey. Translated by T.E. Shaw. New York: Oxford University Press, 1935.

Odyssey. Translated by W.H.D. Rouse. New York: New American Library, 1949.

Odyssey. Translated by E.V. Rieu. Baltimore: Penguin Books, 1961.

Odyssey. Translated by Robert Fitzgerald. New York: Anchor-Doubleday, 1962.

Odyssey. Translated by Richmond Lattimore. New York: Harper, 1965.

Odyssey. Translated by Albert Cook. New York: Norton, 1967.

Editor's Note: In a poll conducted in the 1980s of seventy-eight professors then teaching Homer in well-known colleges and universities, more than three-quarters of the respondents indicated their preference for the 1951 Lattimore translation of the *Iliad*; Robert Fitzgerald's and E.V. Rieu's versions scored second and third place, respectively. Regarding the *Odyssey*, most preferred Fitzgerald's translation, with Lattimore's and Rieu's versions tied for second place. The other translations listed above are also excellent and widely read.

THE *ILIAD* AND THE *ODYSSEY* RETOLD FOR YOUNGER READERS

Peter Connolly, *The Legend of Odysseus.* New York: Oxford University Press, 1986.

Bernard Evslin, *The Adventures of Ulysses.* New York: Scholastic Book Services, 1969.

Iliad. Retold by Barbara Leonie Picard. New York: Oxford University Press, 1960.

Odyssey. Retold by Barbara Leonie Picard. New York: Oxford University Press, 1952.

ABOUT HOMER, THE *ILIAD*, AND THE *ODYSSEY*

Kenneth Atchity et al., *Critical Essays on Homer.* Boston: G.K. Hall, 1987.

Rachel Bespaloff, *On the Iliad.* New York: Harper Torchbooks, 1947.

C.M. Bowra, *Homer.* New York: Charles Scribner's Sons, 1972.

——, *Traditions and Design in the* Iliad. Oxford: Oxford University Press, 1930.

Ernle Bradford, *Ulysses Found.* New York: Harcourt, Brace and World, 1963.

Howard W. Clarke, ed., *Twentieth Century Interpretations of the* Odyssey: *A Collection of Critical Essays.* Englewood Cliffs, NJ: Prentice-Hall, 1983.

Jasper Griffin, *Homer on Life and Death.* Oxford: Clarendon Press, 1980.

——, *Homer: The Odyssey.* Cambridge, England: Cambridge University Press, 1987.

G.S. Kirk, *Homer and the Oral Tradition.* Cambridge, England: Cambridge University Press, 1976.

Martin Mueller, *The Iliad.* London: George Allan and Unwin, 1984.

John L. Myres, *Homer and His Critics.* London: Routledge and Kegan Paul, 1958.

Kostas Myrsiades, ed., *Approaches to Teaching Homer's* Iliad *and* Odyssey. New York: Modern Language Association of America, 1987.

L.G. Pocock, *Odyssean Essays.* Oxford: Basil Blackwell, 1965.

James M. Redfield, *Nature and Culture in the* Iliad: *The Tragedy of Hector.* Chicago: University of Chicago Press, 1975.

Seth L. Schein, *The Mortal Hero: An Introduction to Homer's* Iliad. Berkeley and Los Angeles: University of California Press, 1984.

M.S. Silk, *Homer: The Iliad.* Cambridge, England: Cambridge University Press, 1987.

George Steiner and Robert Fagles, eds., *Homer: A Collection of Critical Essays.* Englewood Cliffs, NJ: Prentice-Hall, 1962.

Oliver Taplin, *Homeric Soundings: The Shaping of the* Iliad. Oxford: Oxford University Press, 1992.

C.G. Thomas, ed., *Homer's History: Mycenaean or Dark Age?* New York: Holt, Rinehart and Winston, 1970.

T.B.L. Webster, *From Mycenae to Homer.* New York: W.W. Norton, 1964.

Simone Weil, *The* Iliad, *or the Poem of Force.* Translated by Mary McCarthy. Wallingford, England: Pendle Hill, 1956.

Cedric H. Whitman, *Homer and the Homeric Tradition.* Cambridge, MA: President and Fellows of Harvard College, 1958.

Michael Wood, *In Search of the Trojan War.* New York: New American Library, 1985.

ABOUT ANCIENT GREEK SOCIETY, LITERATURE, MYTHS, RELIGION, AND ARCHAEOLOGY

C.M. Bowra, *The Greek Experience.* New York: New American Library, 1957.

Jan Bremmer, ed., *Interpretations of Greek Mythology.* Totowa, NJ: Barnes and Noble Books, 1986.

Lionel Casson, *The Ancient Mariners.* New York: Macmillan, 1959.

Will Durant, *The Life of Greece.* New York: Simon and Schuster, 1966.

M.I. Finley, *Early Greece: The Bronze and Archaic Ages.* New York: W.W. Norton, 1970.

J. Lesley Fitton, *Discovery of the Greek Bronze Age.* London: British Museum Press, 1995.

Robert Flacelière, *A Literary History of Greece.* Translated by Douglas Garman. Chicago: Aldine Publishing, 1964.

Michael Grant, *Myths of the Greeks and Romans.* New York: New American Library, 1962.

——, *The Rise of the Greeks.* New York: Macmillan, 1987.

——, *The Classical Greeks.* New York: Charles Scribner's Sons, 1989.

Edith Hamilton, *Mythology.* New York: New American Library, 1940.

Herodotus, *The Histories.* Translated by Aubrey de Sélincourt. New York: Penguin Books, 1972.

Max J. Herzberg, *Myths and Their Meanings.* Boston: Allyn and Bacon, n.d.

H.D.F. Kitto, *The Greeks.* Baltimore: Penguin Books, 1951.

Albin Lesky, *A History of Greek Literature.* New York: Thomas Y. Crowell, 1966.

Mark P.O. Morford and Robert J. Lenardon, *Classical Mythology.* New York: Longman, 1985.

Pierre Léveque, *The Birth of Greece.* New York: Harry N. Abrams, 1994.

Don Nardo, *Ancient Greece.* San Diego: Lucent Books, 1994.

——, *Life in Ancient Greece.* San Diego: Lucent Books, 1996.

——, *Greek and Roman Mythology.* San Diego: Lucent Books, 1997.

Plato, *Dialogues,* excerpted in W.H.D. Rouse, trans., *Great Dialogues of Plato.* New York: New American Library, 1956.

Plutarch, *Lives of the Noble Grecians and Romans,* excerpted in *The Rise and Fall of Athens: Nine Greek Lives.* Translated by Ian Scott-Kilvert. New York: Penguin Books, 1960.

Plutarch, *Lives of the Noble Grecians and Romans.* Translated by John Dryden. Chicago: Encyclopaedia Britannica, 1952.

H.J. Rose, *Religion in Greece and Rome.* New York: Harper and Brothers, 1959.

W.H.D. Rouse, *Gods, Heroes and Men of Ancient Greece.* New York: New American Library, 1957.

Michael Shanks, *The Classical Archaeology of Greece.* London: Routledge, 1995.

INDEX

173